In Pursu

In Pursuit of Pepper and Tea

The Story of the
Dutch East India Company

Els M. Jacobs

Netherlands Maritime Museum
Walburg Pers

Cover:
In October 1784, the Amsterdam East Indiaman *Hoop* arrived at the Company's mandatory port of provision at the Cape of Good Hope, halfway between the Netherlands and Asia. Anonymous drawing end of the 18th century

Third edition

Translation: Kist Kilian Communications
Photography of the Netherlands Maritime Museum Collection: Frans Hemelrijk and Thijs Quispel
Design: Jolijn van de Wouw
Printer: Walburg Pers

ISBN 90 5730 040 0

References

L. Blussé and J. de Moor, *Nederlanders overzee. De eerste vijftig jaar 1600-1650*, Franeker 1983

J. R. Bruijn, F. S. Gaastra and I. Schöffer ed., *Dutch-Asiatic shipping*, Rijks Geschiedkundige Publicatiën Grote Serie 165-167, The Hague 1979-87

J. R. Bruijn and J. Lucassen ed., *Op de schepen der Oost-Indische Compagnie. Vijf artikelen van J. de Hullu*, Groningen 1980

F. S. Gaastra, *De geschiedenis van de VOC*, 2nd revised edition Zutphen 1991

R. van Gelder and L. Wagenaar, *Sporen van de Compagnie. De VOC in Nederland*, Amsterdam 1988

J. B. Kist ed., *Van VOC tot Werkspoor; het Amsterdamse industrieterrein Oostenburg*, Utrecht 1986

J. J. Steur, *Herstel of ondergang. De voorstellen tot redres van de V.O.C. 1740-1795*, Utrecht 1984

Introduction

The Netherlands Maritime Museum in Amsterdam has been charting a new course. The permanent exhibition offering a chronological overview of the history of Dutch shipping will be reinstalled in stages and organized around various themes. To initiate this reinstallation, in 1992 the Museum will open a 'Company Hall' devoted to the history of the Dutch East India Company. The presentation will concentrate primarily on the maritime aspects of the enterprise. The cultural and economic significance of the Company in the Dutch Republic and daily life in its settlements in Asia will receive less attention.

In addition, a replica of the Dutch East Indiaman *Amsterdam*, moored to the jetty of the Museum, has been open to the public since April 1991. A tour of the ship vividly brings to life the hardships the Dutch suffered in the past in their efforts to obtain exotic products from Asia.

With the new presentation in the Company Hall and the East Indiaman, the Netherlands Maritime Museum seeks to make the history of the world's largest trading and shipping company – which the Dutch East India Company was in the 17th and 18th century – accessible to a broad public.

The Museum would like to express its gratitude to Leiden historian, Els Jacobs. In addition to preparing her dissertation on the Asian branch of the Company, as guest curator she planned the new presentation of the Dutch East India Company, of which *In Pursuit of Pepper and Tea* forms a part.

Hans Bakker,
Director

Contents

7 Origins

15 A Trading Company

23 Company Ships and Shipbuilding

37 Master and Crew

51 Cash and Commodities from Europe

55 The Route to Asia

73 Settlements in Asia

83 Asian Products

91 The Return Fleet

95 The Collapse

Origins

On a spring day in 1594 nine merchants gathered around a table at the wine tavern of Martin Spil in Amsterdam. Hendrik Hudde, Reinier Pauw, Pieter Hasselaar, Arent ten Grootenhuis, Hendrik Buyck, Syvert Sem, Jan Poppen, Jan Karel and Dirck van Os talked over plans for a joint trade voyage to Asia. They had sufficient reasons for considering such an undertaking. During the preceding hundred years Portuguese ships had transported spices to Lisbon via a route past the Cape of Good Hope. These Asian products, primarily pepper, yielded high profits in Europe. In fact, in recent years sales prices on the European markets had increased further due to the difficulties encountered by the Portuguese in bringing their richly laden ships back from Asia safely and on time. They were insufficiently protected against the English privateers who made the waters in the southern region of the Atlantic unsafe. Thanks to the high prices commanded in the spice trade, a great deal of money was to be made: only not by Amsterdam merchants.
The Portuguese king leased his monopoly on the import and sale of spices to exclusive groups of merchants. A so-called 'Indian pepper contract' regulated Asian imports while a 'European contract' determined sales in Lisbon. Under the protection of the Portuguese crown, merchants holding the Indian contract were permitted to buy pepper anywhere in Asia, but were required to deliver the spices to the Portuguese king in Lisbon

The pepper plant is a climbing shrub that winds up around the trunk of a shady tree.
Detail of a print in J. Nieuhof, *Gedenckwaerdige zee- en lantreize*, Amsterdam 1682

for a fixed price. Participants in the European contract purchased the pepper from the Portuguese crown for a higher, pre-determined price and consequently sold the spices at a profit on the open European market. Since 1591, the European pepper contract had been controlled by an international cooperative of powerful bankers and merchants, that had representatives stationed in virtually every large port in Europe. This system allowed them complete and exclusive control over the sale of spices as well as the resulting high profits.

The nine merchants gathered in the Amsterdam wine house wanted to circumvent the international cooperative's authority and make their fortunes in the spice trade. They had sufficient means at their disposal. The starting capital necessary for outfitting several ships for Asia could be collected in no time. A great deal of money was available in the Northern Netherlands as a result of the Baltic grain and wood trade, herring fishing and the export of dairy products and cloth. Furthermore, many wealthy merchants had fled from the Southern Netherlands to the north with all their earthly possessions, when Antwerp fell into Spanish hands in 1585 and the city lost its position as the staple market of northwestern Europe. Jan Karel and Dirck van Os were also Flemish immigrants.

In addition, the merchants had sufficient information. They knew the stories told by Dutchmen, such as Dirck Gerritsz 'China' and Jan Huygen van Linschoten, who had many years of experience working for the Portuguese in Asia. Dirck Gerritsz relayed his information to Lucas Jansz Waghenaer, who included the material in his second large sea atlas *Het thresoor der zeevaert* (The Treasure of Navigation, 1592). Van Linschoten summarized his experiences and extensive knowledge in his *Itinerario* (Itinerary, 1596), which

Jan Huygen van Linschoten was in Asia from 1583 to 1588 in the service of the archbishop of Goa in India. After his return he compiled the first Dutch standard work on Asia.

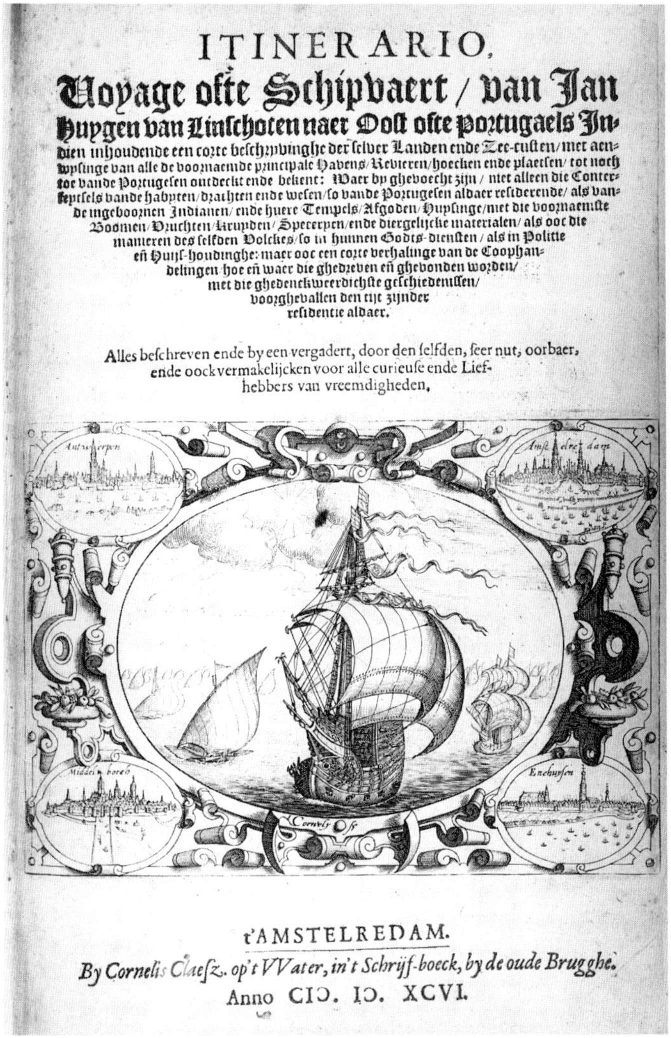
ITINERARIO,
Voyage ofte Schipvaert / van Jan Huygen van Linschoten naer Oost ofte Portugaels Indien inhoudende een corte beschryvinghe der selver Landen ende Zee-custen / met aenwysinge van alle de voornaemde principale Havens / Revieren / hoecken ende plaetsen / tot noch toe vande Portugesen ontdeckt ende bekent: Waer by ghevoecht zijn / niet alleen die Conterfeytsels vande habyten / drachten ende wesen / so vande Portugesen aldaer residerende / als vande ingeboornen Indianen / ende huere Tempels / Afgoden / Huysinge / met die voornaemste Boomen / Vruchten / Kruyden / Speceryen / ende diergelijcke materialen / als ooc die manieren des selfden Volckes / so in hunnen Godts-diensten / als in Politie en Huys-houdinghe: maer ooc een corte verhalinge van de Coophandelingen hoe en waer die ghedreven en ghevonden worden / met die ghedenckweerdichste geschiedenissen / voorghevallen den tijt zijnder residentie aldaer.

Alles beschreven ende by een vergadert, door den selfden, seer nut, oorbaer, ende oock vermakelijcken voor alle curieuse ende Liefhebbers van vreemdigheden,

t'AMSTELREDAM.
By Cornelis Claesz. op't VVater, in't Schrijf-boeck, by de oude Brugghe.
Anno CIↃ. IↃ. XCVI.

Pieter Platvoet (Flat Foot), or Petrus Plancius as he was called in Latin, made a large wall map of Asia in 1592 that he presented to the States-General. This reprint was published around 1602. (Detail)

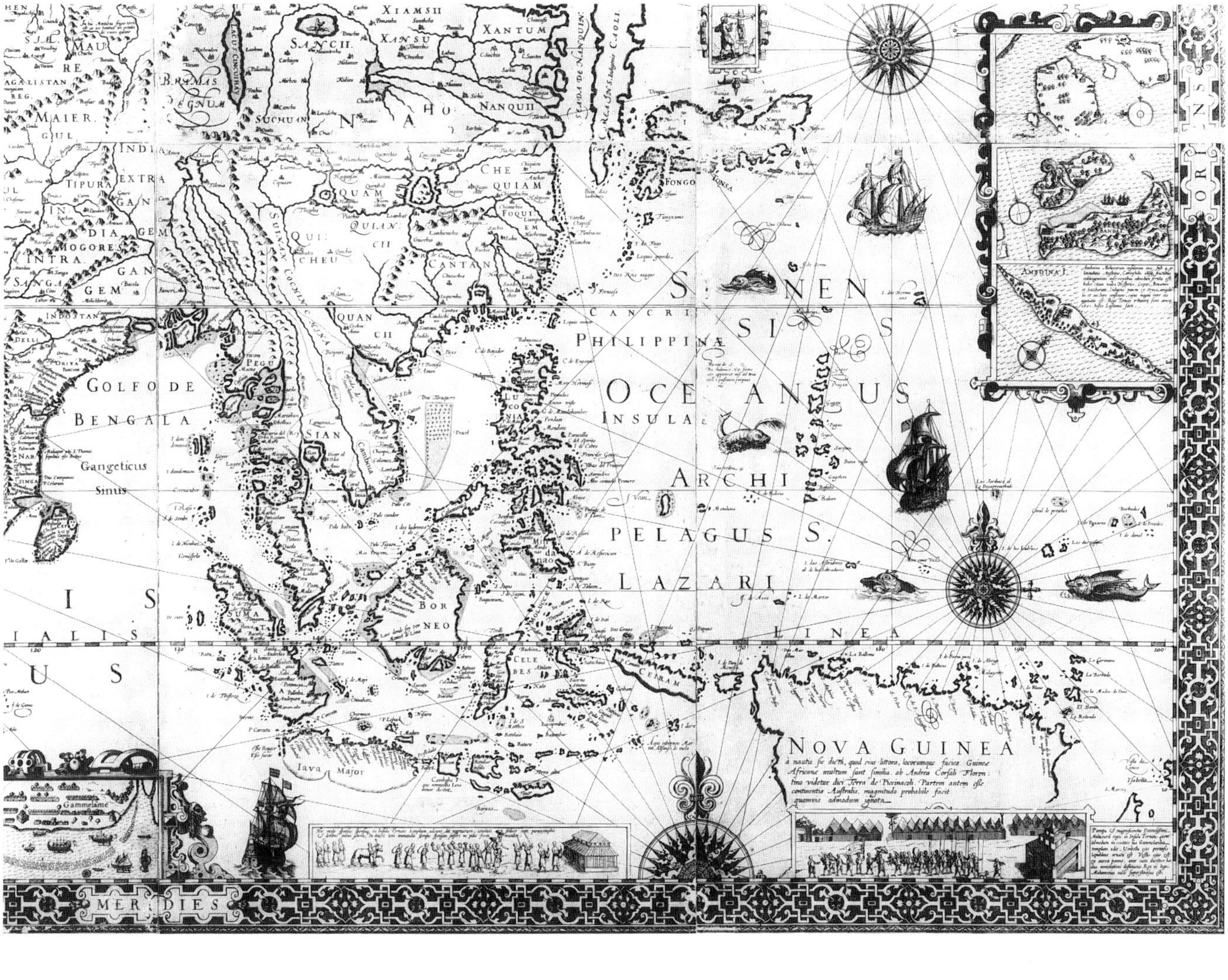

served simultaneously as a seaman's manual, a merchant's guide and a description of Asian countries and people. He provided sailing instructions, detailed descriptions of ports and outlined the existing trade routes in Asia. He also pinpointed the weak areas of the Portuguese organization there. Van Linschoten gave the nine Amsterdam merchants a handwritten version of his *Itinerario* for perusal and the merchants, moreover, sent 'spies' to Lisbon to collect additional information. The learned cartographer and clergyman Petrus Plancius, also a refugee from the Southern Netherlands, integrated all the information into clear and usable instructions and charts.

The merchants briefly debated sending their ships to Asia via the Northern Arctic Ocean. This route seemed much shorter, was safer due to the absence of enemy Portuguese ships and the climate along the way was healthier. Furthermore, they would rupture the Portuguese spice monopoly less conspicuously. After some deliberation, the merchants decided to attempt the route around the Cape of Good Hope nevertheless. They joined forces and established a 'company' for the organization and implementation of their plans. At the time, this was the usual course of action for such ambitious and bold ventures.

The nine merchants personally fronted a substantial portion of the capital necessary for the enterprise and appealed to others to contribute money as well. These less significant contributors were merely shareholders while the nine initiators became the directors of the company. They made the decisions and managed all business matters, bought the merchandise, had the ships built and recruited the crew. For these activities the directors received one percent of the total expense of outfitting the vessels and another one percent of the total profit at the end of the voyage. Once the merchandise was auctioned, the personnel was fired, the ships sold and the company dissolved. All the shareholders received their deposits back plus the profit (or minus the loss). A company was thus established on a temporary basis, lasting only for the duration of one single voyage.

The nine merchants raised almost 300,000 guilders for their 'Far Lands Company'. They spent two-thirds of it on ships, weapons, ammunition, merchandise and recruiting crew. They sent the remainder in cash on board the ships. Several cities, together with the provincial government, the States of Holland, supported the undertaking by supplying more than one hundred guns and smaller weapons free of charge. Import and export duties were waived for the company and Stadholder-Prince Maurits extended patents to the merchants permitting them to legitimize their claims in Asia. After these careful preparations the first expedition to Asia was finally ready. On 2 April 1595 the ships sailed from the roadstead of Texel towards the south. They were the *Mauritius*, *Amsterdam*, *Hollandia* and the small yacht *Duyfken*.

The happy prospects of the voyage, however, soon soured. The merchants had entrusted command of the expedition to Cornelis de Houtman and Gerrit van Beuningen who, as it turned out, were not suited to their task and soon began quarreling. Much of the crew perished en route from scurvy and the ships finally arrived in the roadstead of Bantam on West Java fifteen months later. Because of their thoughtless actions the Dutch came into conflict with the Javanese and De Houtman and Van Beuningen decided to sail on to the Moluccas. Pressured by the crew, however, they had to return when only halfway there. Due to a lack of manpower they abandoned the *Amsterdam* in Asia.

In 1595 four Amsterdam ships sailed to Asia for the first time, bearing a cargo of silver money, Dutch cloth and all sorts of trinkets. Detail of the title page from *Journael van de reyse der Hollandtsche schepen*, Middelburg 1598

The three remaining ships reached the Dutch Republic at the beginning of 1597. Of the original 240 crew members only 87 were still alive. The profit yielded by the return cargo of pepper barely covered the expenses. The first Dutch expedition was decidedly not a commercial success. However, in contrast to the attempts of other merchants, who had sought a route to the Far East via the Northern Arctic Ocean, the Far Lands Company had demonstrated that Dutch shipping to Asia was possible via the Portuguese route around the Cape of Good Hope. This was no small achievement.

Numerous other Dutch ships sailed to Asia in the wake of the Amsterdam company. Between 1595 and 1601 eight different companies dispatched a total of sixty-five ships spread over fifteen fleets. It might almost be called a goldrush for spices. From Amsterdam, Rotterdam, Hoorn, Enkhuizen, Middelburg, Veere and Delft fleets of up to eight ships set sail. Some enterprises were extremely successful, yielding high profits, while others were complete failures. The merchants used the profits from one voyage to finance the next company. However, the overwhelming success soon turned against the enthusiastic entrepreneurs. Dutch merchants began competing fiercely thus driving up the purchase prices in Asia. Conversely, the sales prices in the Dutch Republic fell because of the vast quantities of spices glutting the market. Profits decreased dramatically. The ferocious competition among the merchants threatened to annihilate the economic basis of Dutch trade to Asia. Moreover, outside competitors, Asian, Portuguese, Spanish and English merchants, profited from the discord among the Dutch. Although the Dutch merchants recognised the necessity for cooperation, they remained unwilling to join forces. Some degree of cooperation did evolve between companies within the provinces of Zeeland and Holland. Nevertheless, companies from these provinces continued competing with each other, because merchants from one province were unwilling to dance to the tune of their colleagues elsewhere. The various parties came together only under pressure from the central government of the Dutch Republic, the States-General, and interference on the part of Prince Maurits. The local companies agreed to merge into a single *Verenigde Oostindische Compagnie* (VOC = United Dutch East India Company), which received the monopoly on all Dutch trade and shipping to Asia.

Seven directors were responsible for the daily management of the voc chamber in Hoorn. The 'bankbook' lies on the table. Painting by J. de Baen 1682 (Westfries Museum Hoorn)

Ships of the Zeeland Chamber departed from the roadstead before Fort Rammekens near Flushing. The *Zuiderburg* had a capacity of 1150 tons and sailed to Asia in December 1788. Painting by E. Hoogerheyden 1788

A Trading Company

The special privileges, that the States-General awarded to the united trading enterprise, were laid down on 20 March 1602 in an official charter that remained provisionally valid until 1623. Aside from the sole right to fit out ships for trade east of the Cape of Good Hope or through the Straits of Magellan, the VOC was authorised to wage war and make treaties with Asian rulers, to build fortifications and trading posts, to enlist soldiers and appoint administrators. For a private enterprise such as the VOC these privileges were indeed quite exceptional. The only control the States-General had over their use or abuse was the oath of allegiance the directors of the new Company were required to take. In practice, the directors were free to do as they pleased and could exploit their trade monopoly with powerful means.

In addition to the special rights, the charter determined the precise organization of the united trade enterprise. The former local companies in Amsterdam, Zeeland, Rotterdam, Delft, Hoorn and Enkhuizen became departments or 'chambers' of the new trading company. Governors of the former companies became the new directors of the chambers and local participants became the shareholders of one United East India Company. The essential difference between the previous companies and the new organization was that after the auctions of the Asian return cargoes the personnel was *not* fired and the ships were *not* sold. Furthermore, the directors were no longer personally liable for the Company's debts. Thus, the newly established VOC was no longer simply a temporary venture for a single voyage as the former companies had been, but almost a modern corporate enterprise which, thanks to the various renewals of its charter, was to remain in existence for two centuries.

Collecting capital for the new Company began shortly after the institution of the charter. Each VOC chamber opened a register of shareholders. The total deposits amounted to almost 6.5 million guilders. The Amsterdam Chamber contributed the largest share with 3.7 million guilders, followed by Zeeland which invested 1.3 million. Deposits were much lower in the other chambers, varying from 170,000 guilders in Rotterdam to more than half a million in Enkhuizen.

The capital stock of the VOC was never increased in the course of its existence. Possibly the directors feared a drop in quotations and did not want to drive away existing shareholders. After all, with a greater number of shareholders the dividends would have to be shared by more people. When the Company needed more capital, it simply managed with various sorts of short-term loans, such as one-year obligations and advances. These were paid by merchants to the VOC in anticipation of the first upcoming auction where they planned to buy various Asian products. Besides the interest on the advances, the merchants were given first

'Seeing that the well-being of the United Provinces consists primarily in navigation, trade and commerce', the States-General granted a 'charter to East India' in 1602.

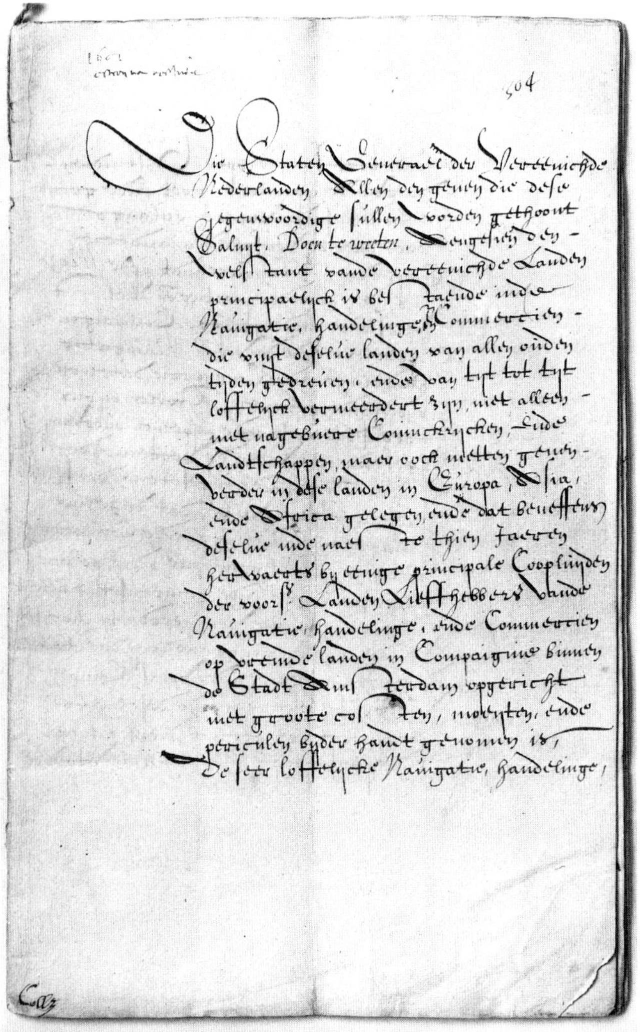

504

Die Staten Generael der Vereenichde
Nederlanden, Allen den genen die dese
jegenwoordige sullen worden getoont
Saluyt. Doen te weten, Dengeenen den -
welstant vande Vereenichde Landen
principaelyck is bestaende inde
Navigatie, handelinge, ende Commercien -
die wt deselve landen van allen ouden
tyden gedreven, ende van tyt tot tyt
loffelyck vermeerdert zyn, niet alleen -
met nagebuere Coninckrycken, ende
Landtschappen, maer oock metten genen -
verder in dese landen in Europa, Asia,
ende Africa gelegen, ende dat benefficien
deselve inde naest te thien jaeren
herwaerts by eenige principale Coopluyden
der voors. Landen Liefhebbers vande
Navigatie, handelinge, ende Commercien
op verde landen in Compaignie binnen
de Stadt Amstelredam opgericht
met groote costen, moeyten, ende
periculen by der handt genomen is,
De sere loffelycke Navigatie, handelinge,

choice at the auctions. Such loans could run up to 20 million guilders. This way of financing trade activities took its toll in times of crisis, such as when the VOC had no goods to auction. The Company faced grave financial difficulties particularly during the Fourth Anglo-Dutch War at the end of the 18th century. The States-General had to bolster it with substantial loans.

As a matter of fact, this was not the first time such measures had been effected. As early as 1610 considerable financial support had been necessary to keep the young VOC on its feet. In exchange for their financial aid, the States-General demanded some authority over business matters within the Company. Through extra-ordinary directors, who, though they did not have voting power, did attend the meetings of the Board of Directors and could keep a close watch, various provinces and cities acquired some say in VOC matters. In times of prosperity and high profit, however, criticism subsided. During the two centuries of its existence, the Company paid 3600 percent in dividends based on the first investment; a sum of more than 230 million guilders.

The very first shareholders were drawn from all levels of Dutch society. Among them were extremely wealthy merchants, including many originally from the Southern Netherlands, who invested 12,000 guilders or more. Also participating in the enterprise were clergymen, craftsmen, wage labourers and simple housemaids. The Haarlem clothpacker Pieter Goossen invested 900 guilders, the spoonmaker Thijs Diercksz 150 guilders, and the Amsterdam wool seamstress Klazien Klaasdr and maidservant Aaltje Gerritsdr each invested 100 guilders. After several years, however, most of the shares fell into the hands of major and minor merchants. Shareholders, just as in the former companies, had no say in the management of the

Company. In contrast to the previous trading companies, however, the voc shareholders' capital was not reimbursed upon completion of a single voyage. As a result they could not make their presence felt by refusing to finance the following voyage. At the beginning of the 17th century, this impotence led to heated conflicts between the shareholders and directors. The participants had no insight into the financial situation, because the directors refused to supply adequate information and dividends were not paid out during the first years of the voc's existence. No wonder they accused the directors of enriching themselves at the Company's expense and they voiced their dissatisfaction in sharply critical pamphlets.

As a result, the contributers secured some influence in matters of policy when the Company's charter was renewed in 1622. They were allowed to elect several principal shareholders representing their interests, who were to establish control boards. A principal shareholder in the Amsterdam or Zeeland Chamber had to own a share worth at least 6000 guilders; those in the other chambers, 3000 guilders. They examined the ten- and, later, four-yearly accounts of the Company and had seats in the electoral colleges, which recommended candidates for vacant director's seats. Henceforth, nine, sworn chief participants attended the meetings of the voc's Board of Directors.

The superiors of the former companies, seventy-six in all, became the new directors. The charter determined that their number had to be decreased to sixty through gradual dismissal. Amsterdam would retain twenty directors, Zeeland twelve and the other chambers seven each. Directors were appointed for life, but their positions were not hereditary. New directors were selected from the principal shareholders of the voc who, depending

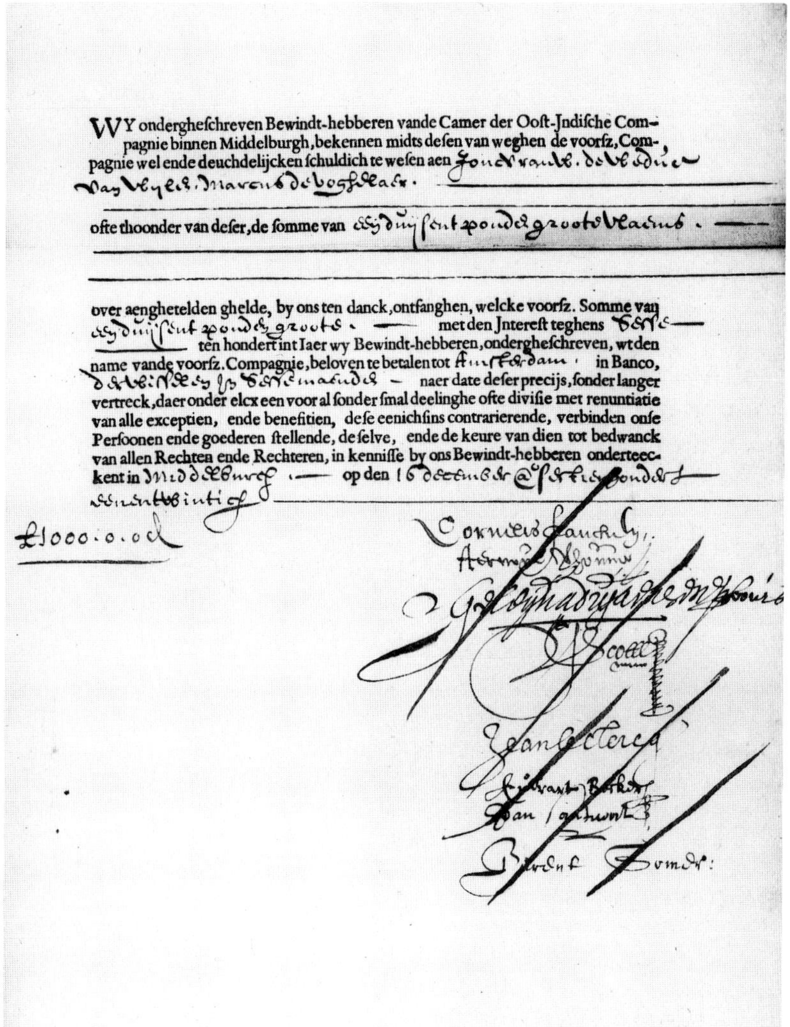

WY ondergheschreven Bewindt-hebberen vande Camer der Oost-Jndische Compagnie binnen Middelburgh, bekennen midts desen van weghen de voorsz, Compagnie wel ende deuchdelijcken schuldich te wesen aen [illegible]

ofte thoonder van deser, de somme van [illegible]

over aenghetelden ghelde, by ons ten danck, ontfanghen, welcke voorsz. Somme van [illegible] met den Jnterest teghens [illegible] ten hondert int Iaer wy Bewindt-hebberen, ondergheschreven, wt den name vande voorsz. Compagnie, beloven te betalen tot Amsterdam in Banco, [illegible] naer date deser precijs, sonder langer vertreck, daer onder elcx een voor al sonder smal deelinghe ofte divisie met renuntiatie van alle exceptien, ende benefitien, dese eenichsins contrarierende, verbinden onse Persoonen ende goederen stellende, deselve, ende de keure van dien tot bedwanck van allen Rechten ende Rechteren, in kennisse by ons Bewindt-hebberen onderteeckent in [illegible] op den 16 december [illegible]

£1000.0.0d

The widow of the late Marcus de Voghelaer, Esquire, received a bond payable to the holder as proof that she had lent the voc 1000 Flemish pounds (6000 guilders) in December 1621.
(Algemeen Rijksarchief The Hague)

on the chamber, had invested 3000 to 6000 guilders. Directors were therefore frequently wealthy merchants and members of distinguished bankers' families, who, moreover, wielded considerable authority in governmental circles of the Dutch Republic. An electoral college, made up of the sitting directors and, later, an equal number of principal shareholders, composed a list of three candidates from which the municipal council of the city, where the chamber was established, made a selection. This policy reinforced the ties between city regents and directors.

The directors decided the daily activities of the VOC chambers. For their efforts, they received, just as in the former companies, one percent of the value of outfitting the ships and another one percent of the proceeds. With this money, however, they also had to pay the auction and warehouse masters, bookkeepers, cashiers and remaining personnel. After protests from shareholders, in 1622 the allocation was reduced to only one percent of the returns. Because such an allowance was particularly susceptible to fraud, the directors received a fixed amount as of 1647. The directors of the Amsterdam Chamber received 3100 guilders annually, in Zeeland 2600 guilders and directors of the other chambers 1200 guilders. Furthermore, the VOC paid substantial reimbursements for travel and lodging expenses. In 1761 the Delft director, Vredenburg, received no less than 4600 guilders as reimbursement for expenses on top of his regular salary. Henceforth, the personnel received their salary directly from the Company.

The directors also established the VOC's general policy. Because of the difficulties involved in arranging meetings and making decisions with all sixty directors present, the charter determined that a council of seventeen directors, composed of

As confidant to Prince Frederik Hendrik and relative of Grand Pensionary Johan de Witt, Director Cornelis de Graeff (1599-1664) was an influential man. Painting by Th. de Keyzer 1633 (Loan Vaderlandsch Fonds Amsterdam)

representatives of the six chambers, would form the Board of Directors. Amsterdam was the largest VOC branch and was allowed eight delegates. Zeeland occupied four seats and the other, much smaller chambers one each. The seventeenth member of the Board of Directors, known as the 'Gentlemen XVII' because of the number of representatives, was to be nominated by Zeeland and the smaller chambers in rotation. In this way the largest chamber, namely that of Amsterdam, was prevented from having a majority of votes in the council. Throughout the negotiations between the former companies, the Zeelanders in particular continually warned against Amsterdam's dominance of the new united enterprise. They attempted to limit the power of the Amsterdam Chamber further by establishing in the charter that the Gentlemen XVII were required to meet alternately six years in Amsterdam and two years in Middelburg in Zeeland. In spite of these provisions, the power of the Amsterdam Chamber was far-reaching and its say in matters was often decisive.

The most important task of the Board was to coordinate the activities of the Company and define policy guidelines. The Gentlemen XVII met three times a year over a period of several weeks. The most important meeting took place in September after the return of the fleet from Asia. At that gathering, the Board fixed the number of ships and men to set sail for Asia the following season. They also made a provisional decision regarding the amount of goods and cash to be sent along with these ships. Furthermore, the Gentlemen XVII determined the dates and conditions for the autumn auctions. A second meeting followed in the early spring, in February or March, when the results of the autumn auctions were known. On the basis of this information the

The Gentlemen XVII met three times a year to determine the general policy of the Company.
Detail of a print in *Histoire abrégée des Provinces Unies des Pays Bas*, Amsterdam 1701

Board calculated the rate of the dividends and formulated the definitive 'call for the return cargo'. This was a detailed list of products the VOC ships were to transport from Asia to the Dutch Republic. During this meeting the Gentlemen XVII also set the dates of the spring auctions, when the Company almost exclusively sold spices. The VOC Board convened its third assembly at the beginning of the summer, at which time the Gentlemen XVII prepared instructions for the Company servants in Asia. In addition, they made provisional decisions concerning the outfitting of the ships, so that the various chambers would have sufficient time to prepare for the departures. However, this summer meeting was dropped from the annual agenda in the middle of the 18th century. The decisions were carried over to the spring or autumn meetings.

Although the Gentlemen XVII only concerned themselves with the general policy of the Company, in the course of time their activities greatly expanded. On the one hand, the VOC developed into a gigantic trading and shipping company with six chambers in the Dutch Republic and almost thirty settlements in Asia, more than a hundred ships and thousands of employees who all had to be managed, supervised and instructed. On the other hand, the Board of Directors tried to gain a stronger hold on daily business matters by overwhelming its servants with a flood of extremely detailed instructions. In order to properly fulfill that task the Gentlemen XVII appointed a permanent secretary or 'counsel' and various special committees. The counsel of the Company handled the incoming letters, suggested replies, drafted the decisions made by the Gentlemen XVII and attended the meetings of the Board. The counsel was a powerful link in the VOC organization since he often held that position for many years, while the directors only attended the meetings of the Gentlemen XVII's as delegates in rotation.

The committees assisted with inspecting the chambers' books or in drawing up financial reports. The most important organ of the Gentlemen XVII was the so-called *Haags Besogne*, which had met in The Hague every spring for four to eight weeks since 1649. Initially this committee consisted of six members, the number later growing to twelve (ten directors and two sworn principal shareholders). Meetings took place in The Hague since Zeeland denied Amsterdam the honour and the Amsterdam directors had little enthusiasm for also rotating committee meetings between Middelburg and Amsterdam. Moreover, the *Besogne* was located close to the States-General in The Hague which made informal and formal consultation over thorny matters easier. The Hague committee was responsible for examining all VOC activities in Asia. This task grew larger as the Asian branch continued to expand. The members of the committee read all the reports and letters sent by Company servants from Asia and checked the correspondence between the VOC settlements in Asia. They reported their findings and recommendations at the meeting of the Gentlemen XVII, who made the final decisions and drew up the definitive instructions.

All the decisions of the Board were then carried out by the various chambers. A fixed division of responsibility was included in the charter to prevent Amsterdam from gaining dominance. The Amsterdam Chamber took on half of all the duties which had to be performed within the newly united company. Zeeland was responsible for a quarter, while Rotterdam, Delft, Hoorn and Enkhuizen were each responsible for a sixteenth. Thus, the former companies developed into six full-fledged VOC departments which eventually all

The East India House in Amsterdam accommodated the offices and auction hall, as well as a slaughterhouse and storage areas for spices. Print by J. van Meurs 1662

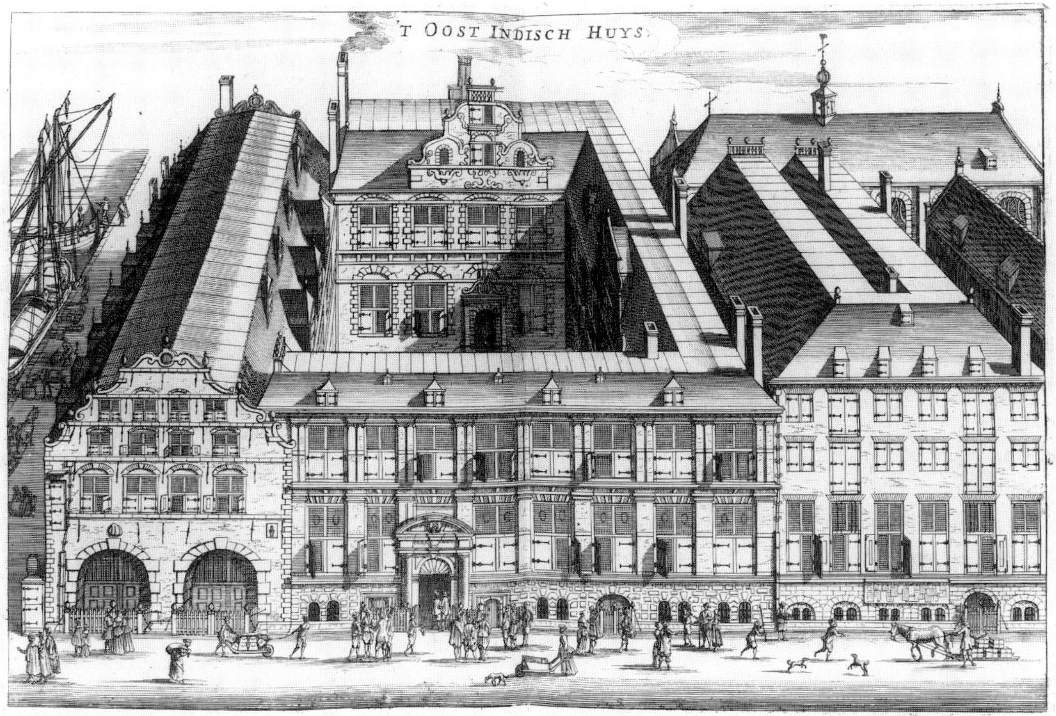

had their own offices, warehouses and shipyards. The centre of local activity was the East India House. It hosted the meetings of the directors and housed the auction hall as well as the offices of the bookkeepers and clerks. In Amsterdam the East India House was located on the corner of the (Oude) Hoogstraat and the Kloveniersburgwal, near the centre of the city. The bookkeepers worked from 7 a.m. to noon and from 3 to 6 p.m. registering cash and commodities destined for Asia as well as the incoming merchandise from Asia. They handled the payroll for both the personnel in Amsterdam and the seafarers and soldiers sailing on Amsterdam ships bound for Asia. They also kept accounts of the expenses for the equipage of the ships. For their work, the bookkeepers earned

1000 to 2000 guilders a year. Clerks in the copy office who wrote out and copied letters and reports day in, day out, received 600 to 800 guilders a year. In the 18th century a total of forty to sixty people were employed in the Amsterdam East India House.

The oldest warehouses of the VOC in Amsterdam were located on the Rapenburg where now – not accidentally – the Peper (pepper) and Foelie (mace) Streets can be found. The scent of all sorts of spices permeated the buildings. A warehouse master supervised the porters who hauled the sacks and bales of spices back and forth. In the attic, 'spice readers' inspected and selected the various sorts and qualities of spices. Around the middle of the 18th century, the Company in Amsterdam employed approximately fifty spice sorters.

Most of the servants worked, however, in the shipyard of the Company. The Amsterdam VOC yard counted more than 1000 workmen in the 18th century and was, in fact, one of the largest businesses in Europe. It was headed by the bookkeeper of the yard. Direct supervision rested with the master of the equipage. He earned 800 guilders per year and lived in a nice house on the wharf. In addition, the VOC provided him with peat and candles to heat and light his house, as well as beer from the VOC warehouses at no charge. When the Company's shipping business expanded in the 18th century, the position of the master of the equipage naturally became more important and his salary was increased to more than 3000 guilders per year.

All VOC servants were directly or indirectly accountable to their superiors, the directors, who shared the various responsibilities. Within the Amsterdam Chamber there were four committees. The Gentlemen of the Warehouse, otherwise known as the Department of Commerce, administered the warehouses and supplies. The Audit Department supervised the bookkeeping, payroll, auctions and shareholders register. The members of the Committee of Revenues were responsible for supervising the cash office and the purchase of gold and silver. The Department of Equipage managed the construction and outfitting of the ships as well as recruiting seamen and soldiers.

The other VOC chambers in the Dutch Republic organized their activities in a similar manner. Their offices, warehouses and shipyards were simply much smaller. On the other hand, the Company as a large trading firm and employer was much more important for the economy of these cities, since equipping a ship bound for Asia required a great deal of effort.

Company Ships and Shipbuilding

In the summer or early spring, after the Gentlemen xvii had provisionally decided the number of ships to depart for Asia, the six chambers were directed to prepare the fleet. The Board set the number of ships on the basis of the desired return cargo from Asia. Because the voc transported its merchandise with its own ships – following the custom of the previous companies – 'preparing the fleet' implied purchasing or building ships. At the beginning of the 17th century the Company, indeed, did buy various merchantmen from private owners, but after a few years it became common practice for the Company to build its own ships. Only after 1780, when the Fourth Anglo-Dutch War created serious problems, did the voc rent several privately-owned ships. The Gentlemen xvii divided the ships among the chambers according to a fixed scheme. Amsterdam supplied half of the total tonnage, Zeeland a quarter, and the other divisions a sixteenth each.

The chambers then ordered the necessary building materials, such as wood, iron, pitch, tar, hemp and flax, almost all of which had to be imported from abroad and were treated in the Dutch Republic. The Company used all sorts and sizes of timber: oak, pine and fir, Koningsberg, Hamburg or Berlin planks, and beams, masts, knees, crooks and floor timber from Norway, Northern Russia and the Baltic. Before construction could begin, the timber first had to be leached in the water near the

Jan Rijksen (1560-1637), who had his own shipyard at the end of the 16th century, later joined the voc as master shipwright.
Print by C. H. Hodges after Rembrandt 1802

shipyard for six months to prevent mould from growing later. In November or December the logs were hauled ashore with windlasses called capstans and moved around the shipyard with a kind of jack and wooden cranes. Wood sawers cut the timber to size and carpenters laid down the keel. Construction of a ship in the yard took approximately three months. This was also the time required for the timber to dry in order to prevent it from shrinking or cracking. The ships were floated in the spring, after which their construction was completed in the 'cage' between the piling in front of the shipyard.

The ships were ready to sail out in September which then allowed time and space in the yard for performing the necessary repairs on the return fleet from Asia. Approximately eighteen months elapsed between the decision to build and the delivery of a VOC ship. Due to the requisite leaching and drying of the timber, construction could hardly have been accelerated.

The master shipwright commanded the shipbuilding. His knowledge and experience guaranteed the seaworthiness of the ships. He judged the wood for quality and usability. He divided the assignments among a large group of ship's carpenters and other labourers he employed or dismissed himself. Naturally, the directors urged him to employ no more workers than were strictly necessary and to get rid of all the 'lazy-bones'. A foreman at the yard had to be an accomplished draughtsman and, in Amsterdam, equally talented married men and residents of the city were given priority over other applicants. In the middle of the 17th century, the master shipwright of the Amsterdam Chamber earned approximately 1000 guilders per year plus free fuel and beer. Skilled ship's carpenters received about 300 guilders annually. They were not permanently employed by the Company, but were hired for fourteen-day periods and discharged 'depending on how the work progressed'. Their daily wage came to 30 stuivers in the summer and 20 stuivers in the winter, when the days were shorter. In the 18th century there was so much work to be done in the VOC shipyards that, in practice, many workers were permanently employed.

During the two centuries of its existence, the VOC built close to 1500 ships. The greatest number of these were launched in the 17th century, while the largest ships were built in the 18th century. After

The large square-stern ship *Parel* (Pearl) of the Amsterdam Chamber was built in the Company shipyard on the Rapenburg. The stern decoration shows a pearl.
Print by R. Nooms 1651

The galliot *Zuilen* set sail for Batavia in October 1658. The Company sold the ship in 1672, after it had made many trips between the VOC settlements in Asia.
Drawing by G. Pompe
17th century

1700 an average of three ships per year were completed in the Amsterdam shipyard. Thus, the Company managed to dispose over a fleet of more than 150 ships. The costs for building and equipping the fleet amounted to approximately 100,000 guilders per ship at the end of the 17th century. The hull cost 65,000 guilders, the masts 3500 guilders, the sails 6000 guilders, the rigging 8600 guilders, the anchors 2300 guilders and the armament 12,800 guilders. In the 18th century the expenses were one-and-a-half times higher. Maintenance following a ship's first voyage to Asia cost 35,000 guilders. Repairs made after the fourth journey could run as high as 62,000 guilders. In the fiscal year 1700-01 the Amsterdam Chamber spent more than 750,000 guilders on shipbuilding materials.

The various types of ships the Company built in its shipyards during the 17th century were not always easily distinguishable from one another. Contemporaries frequently spoke of 'homeward-bounders', but this term applied to all merchantmen that brought goods back from Asia, and did not designate a particular type of ship. Most of the East Indiamen were square-stern ships which, in the 17th century, differed little in appearance from men-of-war. They carried fewer and smaller guns and were furnished with a broader hull for storing merchandise. The wide stern provided extra space for passengers. The large three-masters of the Company varied in length from 130 to 150 feet (37 to 42.5 metres). The length was measured along the lower deck or main deck and expressed in Amsterdam feet measuring 28.3 cm. Between 1625 and 1665 the large shipyards of Amsterdam and Zeeland also built several ships measuring 160 to 170 feet (45 to 48 metres). In addition, smaller square-stern ships, yachts, pinnaces and frigates were laid down. Their length

Three to four hundred ship's carpenters worked in the VOC shipyard in Amsterdam. Print by J. Luyken 1694

varied from 80 to 130 feet (22.5 to 37 metres). In the 17th century the VOC used these smaller vessels for its trade within Asia. They vanished from the Company's fleet in the 18th century.

Besides the square-stern ships, the VOC fleet also boasted various vessels with round sterns, such as fluyts, catbarks, galliots and hookers. The fluyts were somewhat slower than the square-stern ships, but were cheaper to build, maintain and staff and they were ideally suited for the transportation of all sorts of bulk goods. The problem with fluyts was their round stern, which sometimes split under the blazing tropical sun. Catbarks were barely distinguishable from fluyts. Thanks to their straighter boards and flatter bottoms they had greater storage capacity, which also made them clumsy on the open sea. The Gentlemen XVII allowed thirteen to be built in the shipyards of Amsterdam and Hoorn only in the last quarter of the 17th century. Galliots and hookers appeared in the VOC fleet around the middle of the 17th century. These ships were much smaller than the fluyts. They generally had two masts and measured 60 to 90 feet (17 to 25.5 metres) long. These swift vessels were used in wartime and within Asia to maintain communications between the various trading posts and the Dutch Republic.

At the end of the 17th century, the Gentlemen XVII decided to standardise the fleet of the Company further, because VOC servants in Asia complained that it was impossible to deal with the chaotic situation. In 1697, after consultation between the master shipwrights of the six chambers, it was agreed that, henceforth, only three classes or 'rates' of square-stern ships would be built. The largest vessels had to be 160 feet long, 40 feet wide and 17 feet deep, with a capacity of more than 1100 tons. The second charter comprised ships measuring 145 by 36.8 by 15.7 feet or 800 tons. The smallest

The immense East India Entrepot dominated the shipyard complex of the Company in Amsterdam. This small anonymous painting formerly hung on the mantel piece of a voc ropemaker.

The East Indiaman *Gerechtigheid* was launched from the VOC shipyard in Enkhuizen in 1742. The ship had a capacity of 850 tons and made six voyages between the Netherlands and Asia. The model dates from 1761.

Large men-of-war and East Indiamen could only cross the shallows in the Zuider Zee suspended in a floating dock that was towed by Marken fishermen.
Drawing by H. Kobell end of the 18th century

Near the Amsterdam Company shipyard was a section of water screened off by pilings forming a 'cage'. The final construction of the ships, repairs and cleaning took place here. Anonymous drawing 18th century

vessels were 130 by 33.6 by 14.4 feet or approximately 600 tons. In addition, the VOC shipyards would continue to build fluyts and hookers exclusively. These guidelines did lead to greater uniformity of the VOC fleet. However, within a few short years the master shipwrights of Zeeland, Rotterdam and Delft requested a change in the established width. They preferred to build wider ships that rode higher in the water and could hold more cargo. In 1714 the Gentlemen XVII changed the official widths to 42, 39 and 36 feet respectively. However, ships with these measurements proved to be unsafe and slow.

For that reason the Company corrected its instructions in 1742. Simultaneously the Gentlemen XVII tried to introduce a new building method based on the English model, that relied less on the master shipwright's instinct and more on calculations and drawings. The English master shipwright, Charles Bentam, who had already been active for several years in the Amsterdam naval shipyard, produced drawings of the new rates for the VOC. The largest ships measured 150 by 41 by 19 feet; the second rate, 136 by 39 by 17 feet, and the smallest vessels 120 by 33 by 13 feet. Initially, the shipbuilders of the VOC followed their instructions faithfully, but they were not necessarily so scrupulous about Bentam's drawings. It did not take long for criticism to be launched against the agreements. The new ships proved to be poor sailing vessels that made little progress in choppy weather. In 1749 the Gentlemen XVII lengthened the second rate ships to 140 feet and implemented several other alterations that, in fact, made the Company ships swifter sailing vessels.

Although the size of the East Indiamen remained unaltered after these changes, the adaptations of 1749 did not signal the end of the discussion. In 1764 the Zeeland master shipwright, Willem Udemans, proposed that ships be built with three instead of two continuous decks. These three-decker vessels not only offered more living and storage space, but were also safer because the hole or 'waist' between the traditional half decks fore and aft were sealed. In stormy weather, two-decker ships took in treacherous amounts of water in their waist. Opposition within the VOC to the proposal was immediate. Three-deckers were more apt to become hog-backed, and would be rickety, stuffy and insufficiently seaworthy. Moreover, the natural separation, the waist, between the crew fore and the officers aft would be lost. That would have disastrous consequences for the maintenance of discipline on board. Udemans and, later, his son kept hammering away on the advantages and built several three-deckers for the Zeeland Chamber at the end of the 1760s. The ships were a success, but the other chambers refused to follow Zeeland's example. After endless discussion in the 1770s, the Gentlemen XVII granted the chambers a free hand. Only in 1793, when the three-deckers had proven their usefulness, did the Board require all the chambers to build such ships exclusively.

The introduction of another improvement also took years to implement. In 1761 the British Navy began experimenting with the so-called 'coppering' of its ships. An extra sheeting made of copper plates prevented accretion of algae and protected the vessels from pileworm. The ships sailed faster, required less maintenance and had a longer life span. The great disadvantages were the high costs and the fragility of the sheets. A long discussion over the advantages and disadvantages arose within the VOC as well as the Dutch Navy. Finally, the Gentlemen XVII requested the chambers in 1792 to copper all new ships from then on, but because of the high costs involved did not make this mandatory.

Floating a ship in water was a special event. The launching of the VOC hooker *Zon* was postponed until Stadholder-Prince Willem V's visit to Amsterdam.
Print by R. Vinkeles 1768

A third change within the VOC fleet progressed much more smoothly under pressure from the Dutch Government. During the Fourth Anglo-Dutch War, the States-General sent a squadron to Asia under the command of Jan Pieter van Braam to support the VOC's position and power. The presence of Dutch warships in Asia confronted governmental and military authorities with the defective communication system between Asia and the Dutch Republic. When, shortly after the war, dissension occurred with the Spaniards over trade in the Philippines, the States-General made an urgent appeal to the VOC to deploy packet boats to improve communication. Considering the tremendous amount of state support the Company had received since the war, it could hardly refuse this request. Packet boats were cutters built for speed with a single mast with fore-and-aft rigging. They measured approximately 80 feet long with a capacity of 120 tons. Packet boats owed their name to the function they fulfilled. They carried letters, packages and passengers four times a year from the Dutch Republic to Batavia and twice a year to Ceylon. In 1788 the VOC built ten packet boats which, despite the disappointing income from the transport of post and passengers, sailed to Asia on a fixed schedule until the mid-1790s.

The VOC commanded a network of vast shipyards in the Dutch Republic for the construction and maintenance of its enormous fleet. The largest site was located in Amsterdam. Initially the Company had rented and purchased buildings scattered throughout the city. However, around the middle of the 17th century, the Amsterdam Chamber was bursting at the seams in all respects. The shipyard on the Rapenburg, where the oldest warehouses were also located, had become far too small. Fortunately, the vast city expansion of the 1650s provided a solution. In the far northeastern corner on the banks of the IJ, the Admiralty of Amsterdam planned to build a large arsenal on the new man-made island of Kattenburg. A second island, Wittenburg, was reserved for small private docks. The VOC was able to acquire a large part of the third island, Oostenburg, in 1661. In the years that followed the Company built a complete shipyard complex with three large slipways on the IJ side plus a large number of simple wooden workshops and storage areas.

Dominating the site was the four-story VOC entrepot. The building was designed by Daniel Stalpaert, who was also the architect of the Naval Entrepot on Kattenburg, with which the Company building to this day is frequently confused. The ground floor accommodated depots for iron, nails and cables as well as a large slaughterhouse where, in the 18th century, as many as fifty to sixty carcasses could be hung at the same time. The meat served as provisions for the crew on the ships. Higher up in the building were attics for pepper and other spices, all sorts of ship-related materials, as well as a sailmaker's workshop which, however, moved to its own quarters on the Oosterburgerdwarsstraat in the 18th century. The VOC entrepot was visible from a distance and made a great impression on contemporaries. Joan Pluimer's poem composed at the beginning of the 18th century lauds it as follows: 'Oh Royal building of the Indies' company, Treasure of the East...and glory of the river IJ...when friend and foe behold your roofs, one cheers while the other quakes before your awesome power'.

Behind the VOC entrepot were located the carpenters' workshops, a sawmill and wood kiln where the boards for the ship's planking were bent into the desired shape. The master of the equipage and master shipwright had their Company houses on the site. The five-hundred metre long ropewalks of the VOC and the Admiralty were built next to each other on a separate fourth island near Oostenburg. In a remote corner, at a safe distance from the other buildings, was the Company tarring house, where ropes were impregnated with boiling tar and where rosin, a kind of boat varnish, was produced. The VOC was only allowed to establish an anchor forge on its site, with no less than eighteen furnaces, at the beginning of the 18th century, because of the opposition of the Amsterdam blacksmiths' guild to such competition. The anchors were tested for quality outside the forge. Dock workers would hoist the new anchors several metres above the ground and then drop them onto a heavy piece of iron. If the anchors survived this trial without suffering great damage, they received the seal of approval. Elsewhere on the complex were four more large warehouses, which were joined together in the 18th century to make one vast building with a courtyard. They were used for storing goods, such as coffee, tin and sugar.

On board, guns made of bronze rather than iron were placed near the helm so that the compasses would not be affected. This bronze cannon for balls weighing six pounds dates from 1695.
Find from the wreck of the *Hollandia* 1743

When repairs to or construction of an East Indiaman were complete, the master of the equipage, master shipwright and ship's master jointly inspected the ship. The names of new ships were determined by the Gentlemen XVII based on recommendations made by the chambers, where directors could submit their proposals in rotation. Wives (*Vrouwe Maria Jacoba*), daughters (*Juffrouw Johanna*) and country estates (*Hof niet altijd zomer*) were conventional choices. The ship was towed from between the piling after its inspection and set off for the roadstead. From Amsterdam, Hoorn and Enkhuizen the ships sailed across the Zuider Zee to Texel and dropped anchor in the Muscovite or Coopvaerders Roadstead southeast of the island. The Zuider Zee route was fairly dangerous. Narrow channels and large, constantly shifting shoals hindered a smooth crossing. Pilots and a precise buoyage indicated the course. For passing large shallows, such as Pampus near Amsterdam and the Enkhuizen Sands, the East Indiamen had to use ship's camels. These were a type of floating dock which were sunk down around the ship and then pumped empty. Suspended in the camel, the East Indiamen were towed over the greatest obstacles by water ships. It was crucial that the large merchantmen did not become cambered or hog-backed during this manoeuvre. VOC ships of

Joan Nicolaus Derck made the ship's bell for the East Indiaman *Vrouwe Maria Jacoba*, that sailed from Hoorn to Batavia in the summer of 1767 under the command of Klaas Ariensz.

In 1768 the directors drank a toast with this specially engraved wine glass, wishing 'a safe voyage for the ship 't *Loo*', that remained in service for no less than 22 years.

the Rotterdam and Delft Chambers had to follow a long route over various rivers and inland waterways to the roadstead of Goeree, because the mouth of the Meuse River was too shallow for the large East Indiamen. From Middelburg the ships sailed via the Welsingen Canal to the Westerschelde River, dropping anchor in the roadstead near Fort Rammekens.
The directors of the Department of the Equipage sailed especially from Amsterdam to Texel, or from Delft to Goeree, to deliver official letters and instructions as a form of final inspection. For this purpose the chambers had swift official yachts with a regular crew, waiting and moored to their docks. These little trips in the chilly spring and autumn were not entirely popular with the directors. After the visit of the local directors the ships could set sail on the next favourable wind. They left the roadstead in groups of two to five East Indiamen flying the VOC banner, though not until the crew and cargo had also been brought on board.

Master and Crew

During the two centuries of the voc's existence more than one million people sailed as passenger, craftsman, soldier or seaman on its Asian-bound vessels. The passengers formed the smallest group of ten to twenty people per ship. They were high-ranking voc officials – managers, merchants, judges or clergymen – going to work for the Company in Asia. They were not required to work on board, were assigned their own cabin on the stern and dined with the officers. These high-ranking officials frequently brought along their wives, children and servants. Other passengers included Dutch colonists who had received permission from the Company to settle as freemen in South Africa or on Java. The voc hoped to stimulate the production of food in this way, particularly on the Cape of Good Hope. Another small group was comprised of craftsmen, blacksmiths, coopers, carpenters or sailmakers who also went to work in Asia in the service of the Company. One-fifth to one-third of those on board were soldiers, hired to guard the Asian settlements of the voc. At the beginning of the 17th century the Company employed more than 3000 soldiers. By 1750 the number had increased to almost 17,000. On board the ships, the craftsmen and soldiers were limited to carrying out repairs, standing watches or serving the guns.

The largest group of people on board were the seamen, from master to ship's boy. The average complement of a voc ship sailing to Asia was 200. This was a larger number than was strictly necessary for a safe crossing. However, the East Indiamen also brought reserve crewmen to Asia for the return voyage and the voc fleet active within Asia. This was necessary to prevent a reduction of manpower due to death. On a homeward-bound voyage there was only an average of 110 seafarers on board. The Company employed approximately 3500 seamen at the beginning of the 17th century. Around 1750 this number had risen to more than 12,000.

The master wielded high command on board. His

A voc soldier kept his cartridges, each consisting of a bullet and a little bag of gunpowder, in a special case. This decorated brass cartridge case must have been the property of a junior officer. Find from the wreck of the *Amsterdam* 1749

most important duty was to comply with and carry out the directors' instructions and assignments. This was no easy task. In the course of time these instructions increased not only in number, but especially in scope and detail. In general the master was expected to maintain order and strict discipline on board. He had the final responsibility for navigation, however, in determining the course he was required to take into consideration the 'sentiment' of the mates. In addition to the first, second and third mates the master received support from a senior and a junior merchant as well as a bookkeeper. Numerous junior officers, all with assistants, fulfilled various specific functions. The steward supervised the distribution of drink and comestibles. The provost maintained law and order.

Able and ordinary sailors, youngsters and boys represented the majority of the crew. Almost all of them were born into the lower levels of society or had been raised in orphanages. Many of them, a quarter to one-half, came from abroad, usually from Scandinavia or Germany. The percentage of VOC soldiers from other countries was even higher. Seamen only elected to work for the VOC out of sheer necessity and the hope of making their fortunes in Asia, because work conditions were poor in the Company. The navy and the army paid their seamen and soldiers the same salary, however the merchant navy extended far higher wages. A VOC soldier earned 9 guilders per month and sailors 7 to 12 guilders, which they could exchange at an unfavourable rate in Asia or else cash at the end of their term of employment. Excluding fines and various other expenditures en route, a seaman was left with an average of 100 guilders per year. In contrast to professions on land, seafarers did enjoy room and board for approximately 70 guilders a year. However, wages for comparable professions in the Dutch Republic were at the same level as that earned by the second mate. In addition, the VOC required mandatory employment for a period of five years, excluding the voyage to and from Asia, while seamen signed up with the merchant navy per trip or per season. Furthermore, the risks entailed during a protracted term of employment under the blazing tropical sun were far greater.

On the other hand, the fixed contract guaranteed a seaman a long period of room and board and some degree of security for his family because, upon the seaman's request, the Company would pay part of

Crew members relieved themselves by hanging half overboard on the bow, the officers did the same on the stern. The (female) passengers, however, preferred to use a chamber pot.
Find from the wreck of the *Hollandia* 1743

This tobacco box, which belonged to one of the people on board the VOC ship *Hollandia*, is decorated with portraits of Luther and the pope who turn into two jesters – when the box is turned upside down.

his earnings to those who stayed behind in the Dutch Republic. Moreover, it was possible to advance and climb the social ladder during the five-year VOC term of employment. Famous examples of this are Anthony van Diemen, Reinier de Klerk and the German, Johannes Thedens, who left the Dutch Republic either as sailor or soldier, ultimately serving as governor-general, the most important Company position in Asia. Despite career opportunities, seafarers did not consider sailing for the VOC appealing and, as a result, the Company had to make do with unhealthy and untrained personnel, including 'all sorts of krauts, bumpkins, clodhoppers, haymakers and other raw kashoobs with grass still stuck between their teeth'. In the 18th century the problem of acquiring personnel became increasingly troublesome. While the VOC required ever greater numbers of seamen and soldiers, the population growth in the Dutch Republic was stagnating and in the coastal provinces the number of inhabitants was even decreasing.

The Company recruited its seafarers and soldiers on fixed days of the year. The directors of the Department of the Equipage held sessions to conclude contracts with new employees. Most of the candidates were escorted to the East India House by a broker who had provided them with room and board. The Company made grateful use of these private agents and their reservoir of prospective applicants. These innkeepers had a special interest in signing on as many possible unemployed guests. Foreign sailors also found work in this way in an alien port. However, the brokers had a bad reputation. They abused the unemployed seaman's unfortunate circumstances. By providing him with room and board and, after he signed on, with a scantily filled sea chest, the seaman was placed under a serious burden of debt. The seaman could pay off a small part with the two months' wages he received as 'press money' when he signed on. The remainder had to be guaranteed with his signature on a so-called *ceel*, a bond acknowledging debt for a maximum of 150 guilders. The Company paid out the money only when the seaman had actually earned it. An innkeeper did not have enough capital to wait that long. After all, a sailor earning 12 guilders a month would not be able to save 150 guilders in record time. Therefore, the innkeepers sold the bond of debt to third parties for a lower sum. They, thus, sold the *ceel* – which sounds like soul – of a

Until 1742 every VOC sailor was permitted to bring his personal belongings on board in a small sea chest. Thereafter, seven men had to share one large trunk. Finds from the wrecks of various East Indiamen

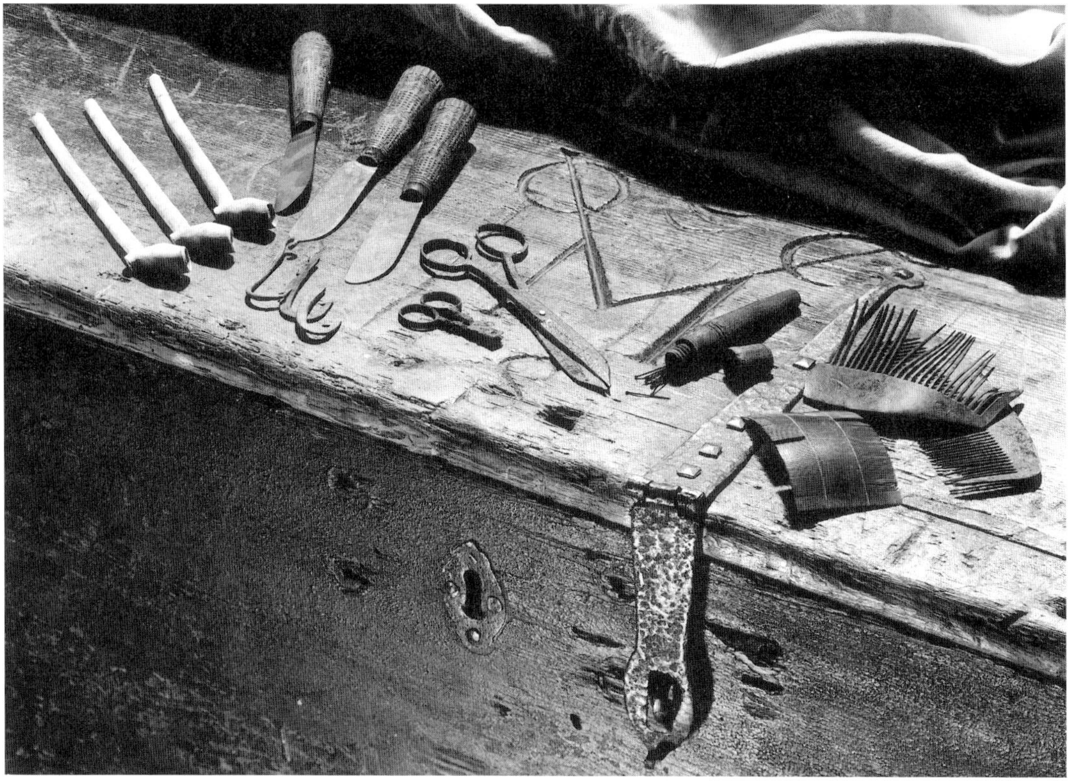

sailor and therefore they became known as 'soul-sellers'.
The voc term of employment – and by extension the earnings – of the majority of the crew officially began when a Company ship left the roadstead and sailed to sea. Prior to that time, a small nucleus of sailors would bring the ship from the harbour to the roadstead of Texel, Goeree or Rammekens. The rest of the crew were transported later in lighters. Their luggage consisted of clothing, cutlery and extra provisions for the first weeks on board. Trousers, shirts, caps, a plate, mug, knife, comb, soap, mirror, box containing tobacco, pipes, tinderbox for lighting a fire, a mattress or hammock, blankets, sheets, pillow-cases and a pillow filled their sea chests. Some brought along a Bible or navigation manual, pens, paper and ink, checkers or chess, flute or fiddle. The extra provisions consisted of treacle, cheese, ham, brandy or beer. Several days before departure, directors boarded the ships to administer the crew an oath of allegiance to the Company and remind them of their duty, as established in the contract agreed to by the voc and the seamen.
Several weeks could pass before a favourable wind blew the ships out to sea. During the wait, and also later on the high sea, friction could arise among the small community on board: between officers and crew, between Dutchmen, Germans, Scandinavians and, in the second half of the 18th century, Asians and between sailors and soldiers. Homosexual relationships or 'sodomy', which was prohibited, could cause turmoil. The presence of female passengers sometimes kindled resentment. Crafty girls who sailed as ordinary seamen in order to be with their husbands in Asia, were firmly dealt with by the Company once they were found out. After all, women were not employed by the voc. Two exceptions were the 'maid of the Chamber' at Enkhuizen who cleaned the East India House, and the cleaning lady on the Rotterdam Chamber's yacht.
A breach of the rules on board was severely punished with fines, solitary confinement on a diet of bread and water, corporal punishment and even death. The most serious violations were mutiny, sodomy and murder. The perpetrators were thrown over board alive, either alone or tied to the body of their victim. Branding, flogging or 'booting', and keelhauling were punishments with less fatal consequences. If a crew member had threatened a colleague with a knife, his hand was pinned to the mast with the knife and he had to free himself by pulling it through his palm. For fighting and the bringing of dice, playing cards and other games of chance on board, the voc submitted the seafarers to a diet of bread and water lasting several days. For blasphemy, drunkenness, throwing victuals overboard, or defecating and urinating in unauthorised areas, the offender was fined two months wages. The same applied to officers who neglected their duty in checking up on sanitation.
The Company devoted much attention to hygiene on board the ships in order to prevent illness and death among the crew as much as possible. The Gentlemen XVII gave clear instructions to air the ship's hold regularly, smoke it out with gunpowder and juniper berries and sprinkle the area with vinegar. The bedding in the berths had to be aired out on deck and the between-decks had to be hosed down. During bad weather, however, such instructions could not be carried out. When this occurred, the hatches and portholes used for ventilation remained closed. Even in good weather the main deck, where most of the crew was lodged, inevitably became a mess. Living there

Master and passengers frequently travelled overland to the roadstead where the East Indiaman was anchored. They were ferried to the ship in sloops.
Detail of a painting by A. Willaerts 1627

Company servants of the Amsterdam Chamber would gather at the Montelbaans Tower in order to be brought to the roadstead of Texel in lighters.
Painting by A. Storck end of the 17th century (Amsterdams Historisch Museum)

Master Dirk Muller (1758-1834), represented in VOC uniform, sailed to Batavia on the East Indiaman *Zeepaard* in May 1788 and returned more than three years later with the ship *Beverwijk*. Anonymous painting end of the 18th century

A notebook such as this one, made of shark's skin with silver mounting, must have been the property of a high-ranking VOC official. It may have been a business gift from the directors (1793).

The activities of the seamen included operating the sails, rudder and the pumps to keep the ship dry.
Detail of a painting by A. Storck 1698

were 200 to 300 seamen and soldiers, with their meagre luggage in chests, crammed together between the hammocks, mattresses and guns. Contaminated water in the bottom of the ship, the crewmen's body odour and forbidden excrement hidden in out-of-the-way corners produced stuffy and musty air below deck.

Such conditions were a breeding ground for disease. A typhus epidemic was capable of reducing the crew to half. Dysentery or 'bloody flux' and flu caught while working on deck in bad weather and wearing wet clothes, were also easily transmitted. A separate sick bay was meant to reduce the danger of contamination. A surgeon was responsible for medical treatment. Though not academically trained, he usually had considerable practical experience and was required to take an examination at the East India House prior to departure. The Company also gave special attention to the contents of his medicine chest. Nevertheless, because of the limited medical knowledge at that time, the surgeon was frequently powerless to help. An average of two out of every three VOC servants sailing to Asia did not return to the Dutch Republic. They either died en route or during their term of employment in Asia and were given a seaman's burial. Colleagues carried the deceased, wrapped in his own hammock, three times around the mast. After a short reading from the Bible the body was rolled from a plank over the side. The mortality rate on VOC ships was higher than that on land in the Dutch Republic, but lower than on the ships of other European companies sailing to Asia.

Another leading cause of disease and death on board was the food. A deficiency of vitamins B and C caused beriberi and scurvy. The surgeon tried to combat the symptoms, such as inflamed gums, unquenchable thirst, heart palpitations and paralysis of the legs with lemon juice and brandy. However, he was unable to treat the root of the problem, namely the change of diet. The menu served on board VOC ships contained plenty of calories, but few fats and vitamins. Spoiling and a lack of variety made the food unappetizing. Mornings and evenings the crew was served grits cooked in butter with prunes 'to keep the body open'. The noon meal consisted of yellow peas or beans with salted meat, stockfish or bacon in butter sauce. Often the cook would find grits and peas with a spoiled crust stuck to the inside of a barrel as a consequence of being stored in a hold, where the air was so foul that a candle would not burn there. Every day the sailors were given a small jug (15 cl) of wine and a litre of beer, which,

Salve in little pots and an enema syringe were among the meagre supplies at the surgeon's disposal for combatting illness on board. Finds from the wrecks of various East Indiamen

The daily ration on Monday differed very little from the menu offered on Tuesday. Moreover, in the evening the crew ate 'the day's leftovers'. Regulation from 1793

Maandag.

's morgens	½	mutsje Genever voor ieder man.
	1	emmer Gort voor ieder 100 man.
's middags	2	emmers Groene Erwten voor ieder 100 man
	25	℔ Stokvis voor ieder 100 man.
		Peper, Mostert, Boter, tot ſous maaken.
's avonds	½	mutsje Genever ieder man, en het overgebleeven Eeten.

however, could only be preserved for a limited period of time. Each week the crew received a half pound of butter and five pounds of bread or biscuits. During the voyage every crew member was rationed several cheeses. If the beer spoiled, passengers and crew had to use the water supply on board, which was sufficient for four months and stored in large barrels with a capacity of 600 litres. However, the tropical temperatures en route frequently made the water practically undrinkable as well. The seamen advised holding the tankard in one hand, while pinching shut one's nose with the other, and then sucking the water carefully through clenched teeth to keep from swallowing the teeming worms infesting the water. If a sailor had lost his teeth because of scurvy then, obviously, this advice was not very helpful. Attempts to distill drinking water from sea water at the beginning of the 18th century were successful but not profitable and, because of the fire, dangerous. The amount of firewood necessary to make small amounts of drinking water from gallons of salt water was too great.

The sailors ate in groups or 'messes' of seven from one large dish or mess-kid. The rest of the utensils consisted of wooden bowls and spoons. The officers used tin tableware and took their meals in the great cabin, together with the passengers. They had a far richer diet than the ordinary seamen, including fresh meat and vegetables. The meat came from the livestock, such as pigs and poultry, transported in special pens. Small kitchen gardens on the stern provided fresh vegetables, such as cabbage, onions and horseradish. However, because the roots of the plants damaged the ships, the gardens were prohibited in 1677.

The VOC crew thus subsisted on an unbalanced diet, lived on crowded, unkempt ships and worked in heavy southwesters and under a blazing tropical sun. Divided into messes and three watches, the seamen were on duty four hours and off eight. In their 'free time' they rested in their hammocks or entertained themselves with jokes and pranks, fishing and sometimes writing and reading. The Company made special books available to the crew, such as *De vaste grond des geloofs* (The Bedrock of Faith), *De spiegel der jeugd* (The Mirror of Youth), and *De spiegel der Spaansche tirannye* (The Mirror of the Spanish Tyranny). While chess and checkers were permitted, playing cards or, in other words, 'playing with the Devil's picture book' was not. Jest and comedy were another way of passing time. A favourite prank was the baptism by sea of 'green' sailors. When passing the Scilly Islands, the Portuguese coast or the equator young mariners were thrown three times from the yard into the sea or drenched with a bucketful of water under the watchful eye of Neptune. The young

The master, officers and passengers enjoyed their meals at a richly set table in the cabin.
Finds from the wrecks of various East Indiamen

sailors could buy their way out of this ritual with tokens for drinks. Owing to the excesses and danger involved, the directors prohibited baptisms by sea. As compensation, each mess received a small quantity of French wine. In the smithy's game, other crew members were the victim. A blacksmith used a colleague's rear end as an anvil. With two pieces of wood representing hammer and iron, he would beat the pillow that was meant to protect the 'anvil'. This was an innocent game until the moment when the blacksmith suddenly pulled the pillow away and continued to forge undisturbed to the onlookers' immense, malicious delight.

The VOC crew enjoyed, however, the greatest pleasure on the return voyage. As a form of extra wage, each Company servant was allowed to bring back a chest filled with so-called 'permitted goods' at his own expense. Initially only the total purchase value of the goods was restricted. However, excesses eventually compelled the Gentlemen XVII to limit this authorised private trading. At the end of the 17th century the directors drafted comprehensive regulations, establishing precisely the measurements of the chest, the number and the types of goods. After their arrival in the Dutch Republic, the Company itself sold these private trade goods at its auctions and paid out the profits to its servants. With this money and his wages, a seaman could live like a 'gentleman for six weeks'. Thereafter he sought shelter at the inn of a broker who provided him with room and board until the next scheduled VOC enlistment day.

A seaman who, upon his return, was paid his wages and earned a little extra with private trade could temporarily indulge his every whim and pleasure.
Print by C. Dusart end of the 17th century

Cash and Commodities from Europe

The cargoes, voc ships transported from Europe to Asia, consisted of precious metals, merchandise, commodities and ballast. The selection depended on what merchandise the Company wanted to purchase in Asia. The existing stock of Asian products in the Dutch Republic, prices, and the demand and taste of the European public played a decisive role in the Gentlemen XVII's decision.

The Company transported precious metals to Asia in the form of ingots and coins. Silver bars came from Spanish mines in South America. The majority was intended for the voc settlement in Bengal, where the silver could be converted into Indian rupees which the Company used to buy Bengal goods. The voc ensured that the alloy of the ingots was equal to that of the rupees, so that no silver was lost during the melting process. Gold bars represented a much smaller share of the Company's freight. However, in the second half of the 18th century, shipments, nevertheless, consisted for one-fifth of gold. These ingots were destined for voc offices on the Coromandel Coast, the east coast of India. There, the Company had the gold converted to pagodas in order to buy local products. The silver money brought by voc ships to Asia consisted of large Spanish and Mexican reals of eight, Dutch crowns, ducatoons or *rijders* and smaller coins or 'payment', such as *stuivers* and *schellingen*. The Company could use this currency almost everywhere in Asia. The far smaller quantities of gold ducats found an eager market in India. Moreover, after 1720 the voc shipped thousands of copper *duiten* to Asia. Due to the great demand for precious metals and coins, the Company was one of the most important clients of the mints in the Dutch Republic which, in turn, profited directly from the Dutch export to Asia.

The coins and bars were packed in small sacks and crates and placed in the master's cabin. In the 18th century they represented two-thirds of the Company's outward-bound cargo with an average value of 4.7 million guilders per year. In the 17th century the voc made due with much smaller cargoes of precious metals, valued at an annual average of 1.25 million guilders, because it could also draw on Asian sources. Between 1640 and 1670, for instance, the Company cleared more silver from Japan than Europe. By 1680, however, these Asian sources were no longer accessible and the voc's export of precious metals from Europe rose steadily until it reached a peak of an average 6.6 million guilders a year between 1720 and 1730. The reason for this was not only the loss of Asian sources of currency, but the increased trade and a shift in the assortment of merchandise as well. In the 18th century the voc brought more Indian and Chinese products to the Dutch Republic and these had to be purchased with ready money.

The merchandise in the holds of the outward-bound ships consisted of all sorts of products.

Because European goods were too expensive and undesirable, the VOC could only dispose of a limited amount of merchandise in Asia. The VOC sold European textiles in Japan and Persia and, later, in the 18th century in China, as well as to wealthy merchants in India and Company servants in the Indonesian Archipelago. Linen and woolen fabrics came from Haarlem and Leiden, where the Company had concluded special supply contracts with the textile manufacturers ranging from 70,000 to 100,000 guilders. Moreover, in 1645 these cities each acquired the right to appoint a director to the Amsterdam Chamber, once more underscoring the interests of the Haarlem and Leiden textile industry for the Company, and vice versa. The VOC shipped woolen *polemieten*, *perpetuanen*, *sergen*, *drogetten* and silk *bourattai* to Asia. Other European products for which there was a small market in Asia were French, Spanish and other wines. They were shipped either in large casks or 'leaguers'; the more expensive bottled wines were stored in crates. The VOC also exported various kinds of beer to Asia, as well as lead, red dyes, such as vermilion and cochineal, and mercury for medical purposes (to combat syphilis), assaying precious metals and making mirrors. All sorts of luxury goods and 'Nuremberger trinkets' completed the shipment for Asia.

An important part of the cargo were commodities destined for the Asian branches of the VOC. This consisted of literally every conceivable item that was either unavailable or extravagantly expensive and difficult to find overseas: gear for equipping and repairing the Company ships in Asia, including nails, tacks, anchors, grappling irons, masts, ammunition, guns, cables, ropes, sails and twine, compasses and binnacles; clothing for the seamen; writing materials, such as paper, ink, pens and penknives; copper pots and pans for cooking;

Padded with straw, 252 wine bottles (220 litres) were packed in rows, with the necks and bottoms alternately facing in opposite directions in one crate. Finds from the wreck of the *Vliegend Hart* 1735 (Stedelijk Museum Flushing)

The sandstones for the six-metre high water gate of Fort Batavia had been custom-made in the Dutch Republic. However, they were only placed in position when the portico was built in 1974.
Find from the wreck of the *Batavia* 1629 (Western Australian Museum Perth)

tools, such as jacks, adzes, chisels, pincers, carpenter's squares and masonry trowels, and building materials for Dutch homes and fortresses in Asia. Well-known are the carved stones for the new water gate of Batavia, used as ballast for the East Indiaman *Batavia*, which sank to the bottom of the sea in 1629 and was recovered in the 1970s. When the anchors and cannons did not provide sufficient weight, the Company dumped sand and gravel into the bottom of its ships.

Most goods were only loaded onto the East Indiamen, when they were already in the roadstead in order to allow the ships to be towed along the Zuider Zee and inland waterways with the least possible draught. This was a time-consuming operation. The volume of the Company goods for Asia in the 17th century annually averaged 7500 tons, a figure that doubled in the 18th century. The VOC contracted special lightermen, sworn to work for no other client, who conveyed the commodities from the port to the roadstead. The Amsterdam Chamber had twenty lightermen constantly at work because not only the goods, but the crew as well, had to be ferried out to the roadstead. A commissioner supervised the activities of the lightermen on behalf of the master of the equipage.

The route VOC ships followed to Asia ran through the Channel, or via the 'backway' around Scotland to the south. Vessels heading for Ceylon followed the east coast of Africa from the Cape of Good Hope.

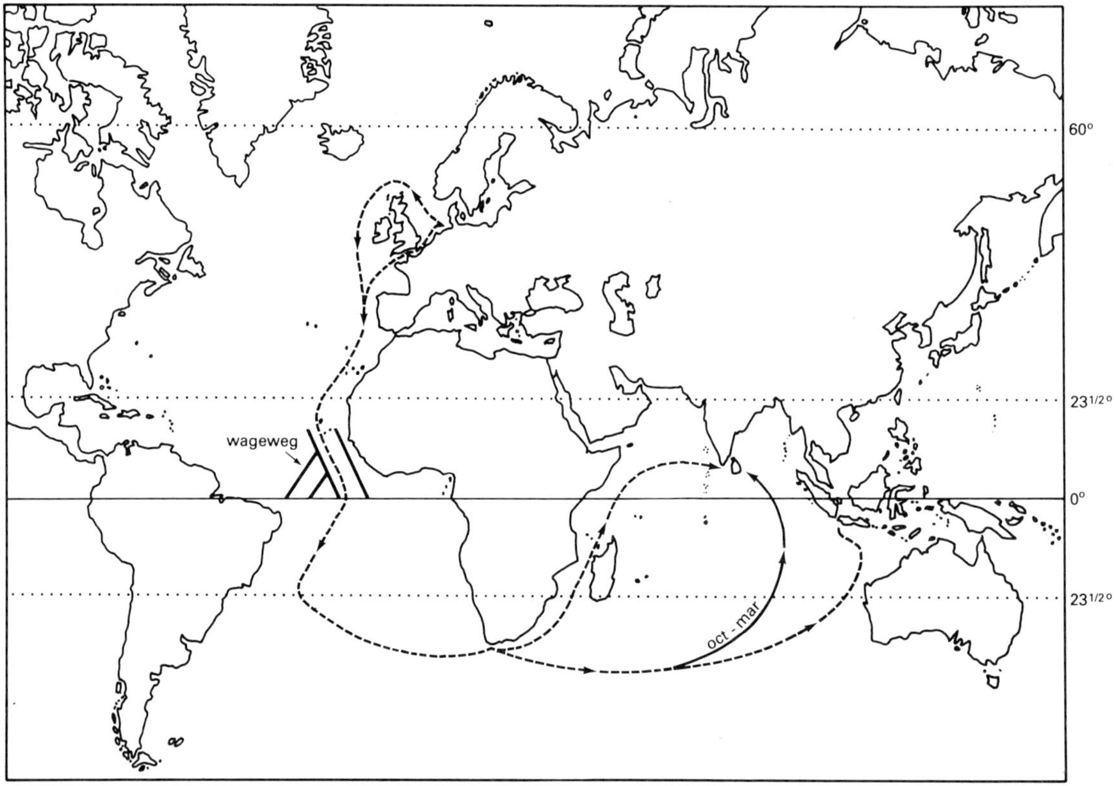

The Route to Asia

Company ships set sail from the roadstead of Texel, Goeree or Rammekens between December-January and April-May. The voc took over this practice from the previous companies. Although the 'Christmas fleet' had to contend with adverse weather conditions in the North Sea, including violent storms and freezing temperatures, it crossed the equator in the right season with the northeastern trade wind blowing full from behind. The ships also reached Batavia, the voc headquarters in Asia, in time to forward the cash and commodities from Europe to the various Company settlements in Asia. In addition, the Christmas fleet departing shortly after the butchering season, could carry freshly salted meat. While the 'Easter fleet' sailed out from the Dutch Republic under better conditions, it arrived in the vicinity of the equator and Asia in an unfavourable season. At the end of the 1620s, moreover, the voc began sending out ships prior to the Christmas fleet in order to improve the connections with Japan, China and India. These ships left the Dutch Republic during the Amsterdam Kermis which took place in September and for this reason was called the 'Kermis fleet'. As the number of ships leaving for Asia increased over the course of time, the dates of departure were spread over the rest of the calendar year.

From the roadstead the voc ships set course in a southwesterly direction towards the English Channel. In wartime, the East Indiamen followed a longer northern route, the 'backway' around Scotland, to avoid enemy English or French warships and privateers in the Channel. The Company ships then sailed south along the Portuguese coast and the Cape Verde Islands. Wind and sea currents determined the route, because 17th and 18th century ships with their square sails could not tack against the wind. In the Atlantic Ocean the East Indiamen had the current of the Canary Islands along the West African coast from behind. If they sailed too close to this coast, they risked being pulled into the Gulf of Guinea by an easterly current. Should Company ships remain too far out at sea then the Southern Equatorial Current threatened to draw the East Indiamen into the Caribbean, where they would endure prolonged doldrums. The voc sought to avoid these predicaments as much as possible. Therefore, as of 1627, the Company marked out a so-called *wageweg* (cart track) on its maps, which the East Indiamen were required to follow from the Cape Verde Islands in order to reduce the risks when crossing the equator. Once in the Southern Hemisphere, the ships sailed along the coast of South America to latitude 30 s, after which they set course in an easterly direction.

The voc ships sailed to South Africa for a mandatory stopover at the Cape of Good Hope, the Company's official supply settlement located 'halfway' between the Netherlands and Asia. The voc built this post in the middle of the 17th

On their way to Asia the East Indiamen sailed between the west coast of Africa and the Cape Verde Islands. This is the northeastern island of Sal.
Drawing by J. P. van Braam end of the 18th century

century, because the ships were unable to take on enough fresh vegetables, meat and water for the months long voyage to Asia. Previously, the East Indiamen called at all sorts of small ports along the route. The Cape Verde Islands, Saint Helena, Madagascar and Mauritius were well-known ports of provision. However, they all had the disadvantage that they only could supply limited amounts of meat, vegetables and water. The growing number of Company ships forced the VOC to seek a better solution. After hearing the description of the Cape's rich possibilities and fertile lands given by shipwrecked survivors of the VOC ship *Haarlem* after an enforced stay there between 1647-48, the Gentlemen XVII decided to build their own permanent supply settlement in South Africa.

A fort with several warehouses, a modest shipyard for repairs and a small hospital were established in Table Bay in the shadow of Table Mountain. The VOC coerced agreements from the local population for the delivery of cattle, laid out gardens for the cultivation of vegetables and fruit, and built a stone gutter to carry water from the mountains to the quay. The directors considered the Cape of Good Hope strictly as a supply station from where the ships were to leave immediately after an eight-day stopover; the time necessary to provision the ships. However, this was not the case in practice. Most VOC ships tarried in Table Bay for four weeks. They used the time to take on fresh food, carry out minor but necessary repairs and, especially, allow ailing seamen to recuperate. Initially the small hospital contained only thirty beds, but at the end of the 17th century the Company built a much larger hospital with more than two hundred places. The rooms were dank and dusty and the VOC had to install bars in the windows to keep the patients from escaping.

To pass the equator, in 1745 the *Vreeland* of the Enkhuizen Chamber followed the 'wageweg' (cart track) marked on the VOC charts. The course is plotted on the chart.
Chart by I. de Graaf 1738

'Cape Town', located at the foot of Table Mountain, became a mandatory port of provision for all voc ships as of 1652.
Pen painting by C. de Mooy 17th century (Amsterdams Historisch Museum)

For healthy crew members and passengers the stay on the Cape, 'the tavern of two seas', was a pleasant recess from the monotony of life on the open seas. Officers frequently sought lodging on shore with freemen who, in the course of time, had settled on the Cape as farmers and small businessmen. A full-fledged city developed in Table Bay in the 18th century, present-day Cape Town. After 1740 the voc also built warehouses, a hospital and other facilities in False Bay, several miles south of Table Bay. Through trial and error the Company had learned that in the winter, when the fierce northwestern storms ravaged the coast, Table Bay was an extremely dangerous anchorage. During a storm in June of 1722 five ships sank and on 21 May 1737 eight heavily laden homeward-bounders were swallowed up by the waves. The Gentlemen XVII determined that from then on Company ships had to anchor in False Bay between May and mid-August.
From the Cape of Good Hope the East Indiamen first set course due south until reaching the latitude 35-40 s. The dominant western winds in that region allowed the voc ships to quickly cross the Indian Ocean to the Indonesian Archipelago. Furthermore, the southern regions were cooler, thus more pleasant for the crew and better for the cargo and provisions. This route was discovered by voc master and, later, governor-general, Hendrik Brouwer, who had tested the seaway as early as 1611 as an alternative for the route along the east coast of Africa or Madagascar used by the former companies. These coasts were riddled with enemy Portuguese settlements and adverse winds delayed the passage.
The Gentlemen XVII made the Brouwer Route mandatory in 1616. After reaching latitude 35-40 s, the East Indiamen were required to sail 1000 miles to the east. Next, the masters had to change tack

The Company marked all ingots with the voc monogram. Between 1728 and 1741 some coins were also provided with a voc inscription.
Finds from the wrecks of various East Indiamen

The Company had all goods and most of the crew transported from the harbour to the roadstead in lighters. Detail of a drawing by G. Groenewegen 1781

Fort Batavia on the Kali Besar (Big River) was the seat of the High Government, the highest governing body of the VOC in Asia.
Painting by A. Beeckman 1656 (Loan Tropenmuseum Amsterdam)

In 1753 the Gentlemen XVII gave their cartographer, Joannes van Keulen, permission to publish VOC chart material as part VI of his sea atlas *De nieuwe groote lichtende zeefakkel*.

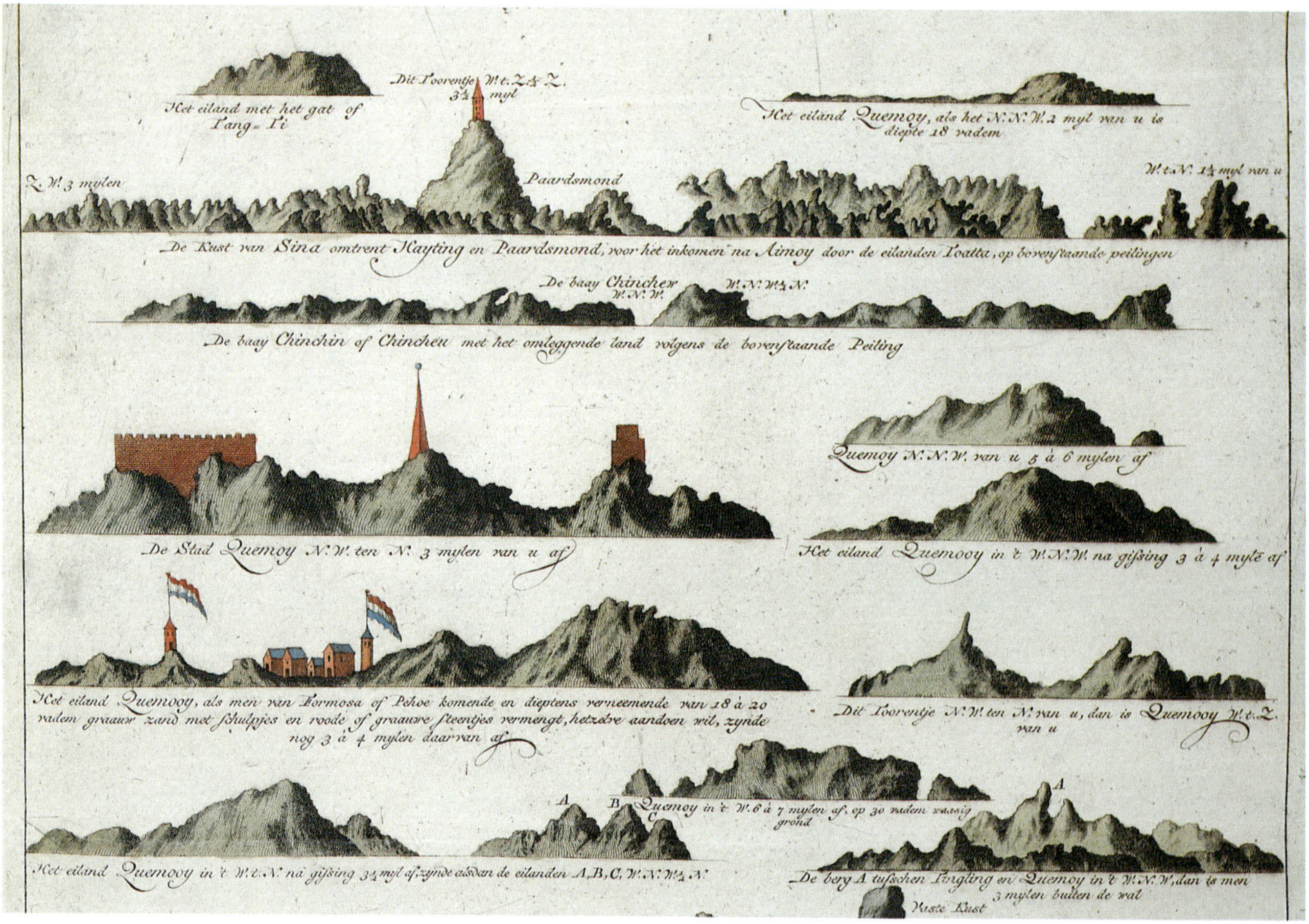

and approach Java in a north-northeasterly direction. Calculating the 1000 miles accurately was not possible until the end of the 18th century. The masters simply had to rely on their experience. They were helped somewhat by sighting the small islands of Saint Paul and Amsterdam, located approximately 700 miles east of the Cape. However, should a master miss these beacons, he ran the risk of turning north prematurely and winding up on the west coast of Sumatra. In that event, it was extremely difficult to tack against the southeast trade wind, raging in that region between April and September, in order to reach the Sunda Strait. If a VOC ship sailed too far east, it ran aground on the west coast of Australia.

This occurred only four times in the history of the VOC, even though Dutch East Indiamen made almost 4800 passages to Asia between 1595 and 1795. Though the risks were great, less than four percent of all voyages ended in shipwreck. A large number of ships ran aground already in Dutch and English coastal waters or, later, in unknown Asian regions. The Indian Ocean was the most dangerous route on the return passage. The homeward-bounders were also more vulnerable. They were (too) heavily laden and either had a minimal European or an inexperienced Asian crew on board. The ships suffered enormously from their stay in tropical waters and their maintenance since their departure from the Dutch Republic was limited to strictly necessary repairs. Given these conditions, the low incidence of accidents is quite remarkable.

It should not be forgotten, however, that the directors took every possible precaution to prevent misfortunes at sea. For instance, the selection of masters was a painstaking process. Candidates were required to have extensive knowledge of seafaring and navigation and had to have sailed to Asia at

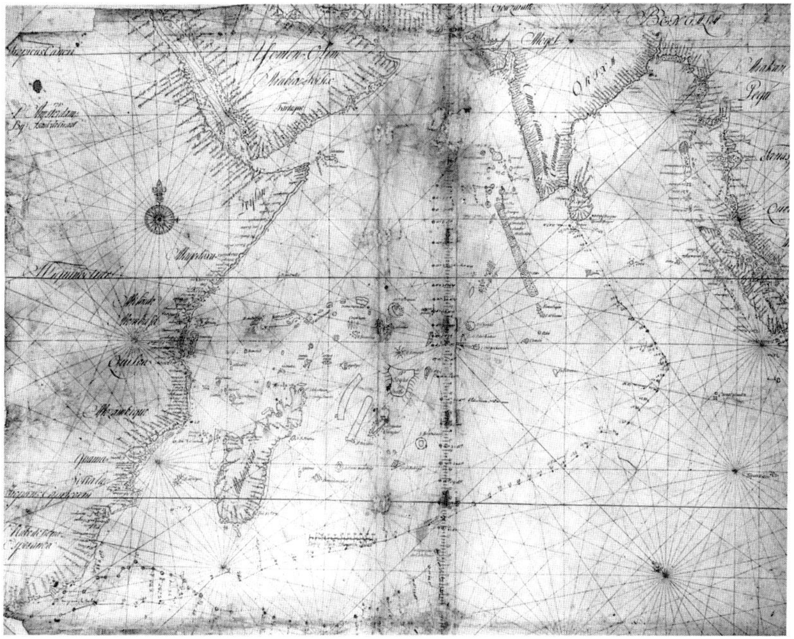

On the Cape, the master of either the *Scheijbeek* or the *Goidschalxoord* handed over this small-scale chart of the Indian Ocean to his colleague on the *Knappenhof*. The routes followed by their ships to and from Ceylon in 1744 have been marked on the charts.
Chart by I. de Graaf 1740

Joan Blaeu (1596-1673) succeeded his father as cartographer of the VOC in 1638. Furthermore, he compiled a beautiful atlas of the world in twelve volumes. Painting by S. van Hoogstraten 1622

least once in the capacity of first mate. This Asian experience weighed so heavily that a seaman with *thirty* years of experience as a master sailing in European waters could only begin with the VOC as a first mate. Furthermore, every prospective master had to pass an oral and written examination covering a wide range of questions on navigation. The directors supplied these able masters with extensive instructions, maps and navigational instruments. The instructions or 'sailing orders' contained detailed information on winds, currents, shoals, towers and hilltops that could be used to determine one's bearings and, of course, the safest and most advantageous route leading past these obstacles and beacons to Asia: *...to sail in the autumn from the Netherlands to Java...*; *...to pass through the Channel with a southwesterly wind...*; *Instructions on the monsoons*; *...on account of taking soundings....* They also dealt with practical matters, such as how to construct a sea anchor or how to pour oil onto the waves during a severe storm. The master used these instructions in combination with an extensive set of sea charts.

The charts were produced in the VOC's own map office. Material used by the previous companies had been based primarily on Portuguese knowledge, however, the Gentlemen XVII established their own hydrographic office with departments in Amsterdam and Batavia. They appointed famous Dutch cartographers, such as Plancius and, later, the Blaeu and Van Keulen families as official VOC cartographers. Their job was to design model charts, copies of which were made for every ship. The Company thus hoped to standardize and control the quality of its chart material. Moreover, the VOC attempted to keep important information secret and prevent it from leaking out to competitors. The maps were therefore drawn rather than printed in order to

The East Indiamen reached Batavia via the Sunda Strait. The ships dropped anchor between the thousands of islands in the sheltered bay before the city.
Chart by G. van Keulen 1714

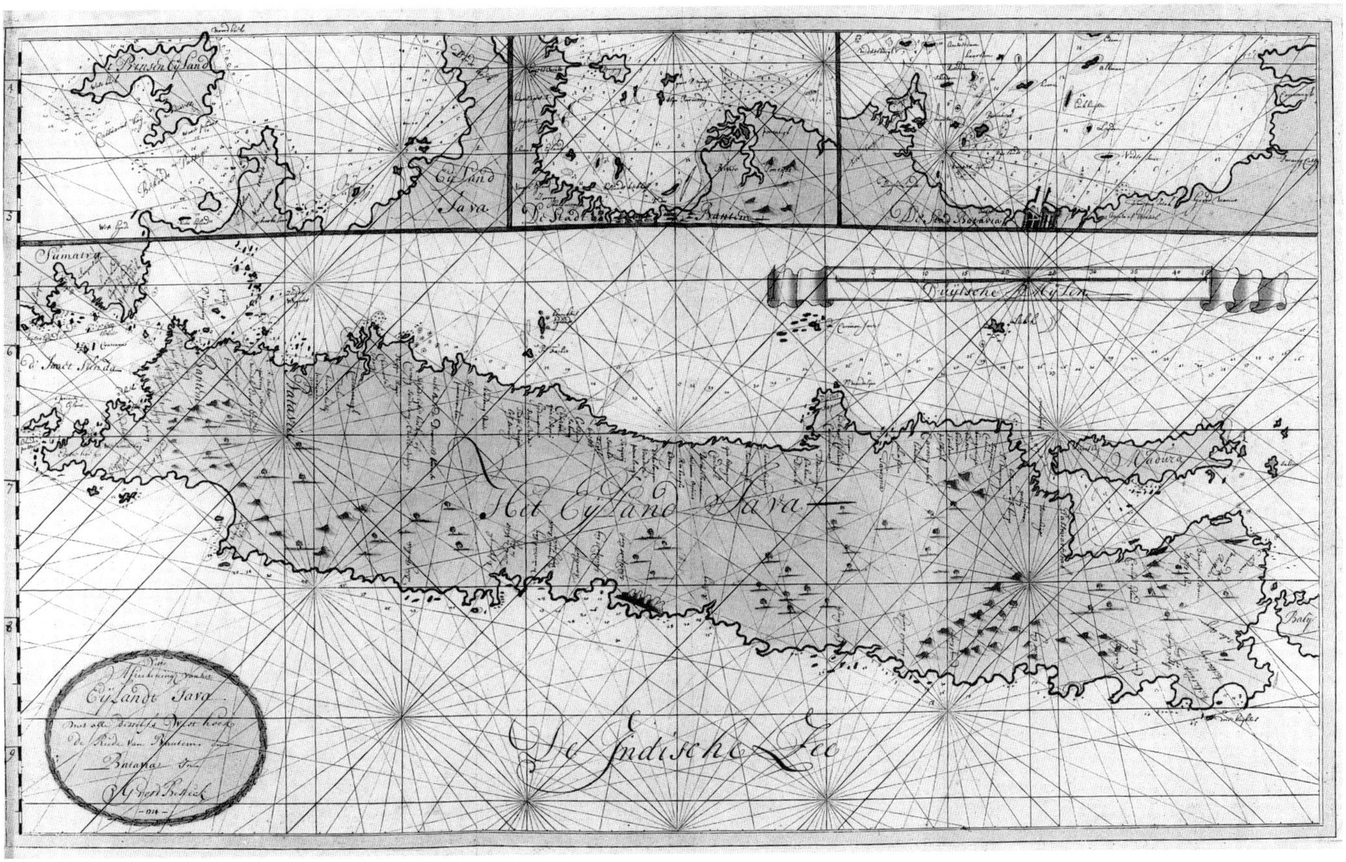

Every VOC ship had twelve dividers on board, three for the master and three for each of the three mates. Eighty dividers were recovered from the wreck of the *Lastdrager* (1653) intended for use in Asia.

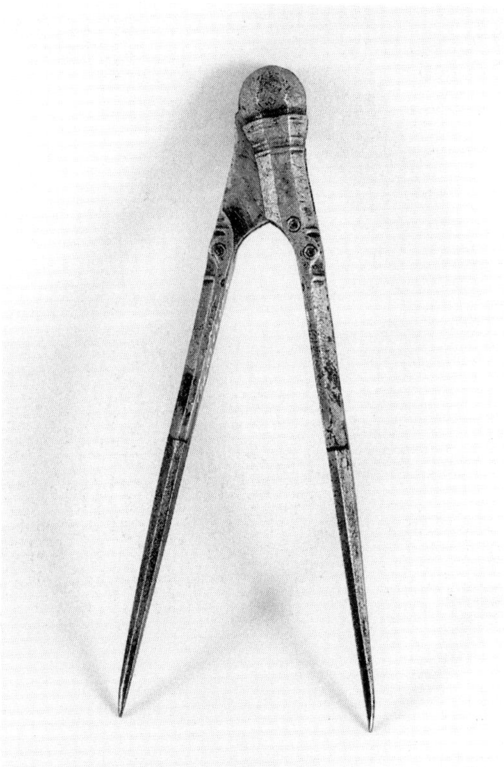

limit production. In addition, it was far easier to correct manuscript charts than printed ones. The Company stored its material in a separate map room in the East India House in Amsterdam, where assistants regularly counted and inventoried them.

When leaving the Dutch Republic the master was issued a complete set of several dozen vellum charts, rolled up in a tin cylinder, plus a variety of sea atlases. Being much more durable than paper and not easily torn, even when wet, vellum was the material of choice for use at sea. The first, second and third mates also received their own sets which, however, contained only small-scale maps of large areas and no detailed maps of coasts and ports. Small-scale charts were used for navigating the route from Texel to the Cape of Good Hope or the Indian Ocean. Only the master had large-scale charts of Table Bay, Sumatra, the Sunda Strait or the north coast of Java between Bantam and Batavia. In addition to these detailed maps, several spare sheets of compass-lined paper were taken along, on which the master and mates could record newly discovered regions or make corrections and improvements. Corrections were related primarily to the geographic longitudes of foreign coasts and shoals. In the past it was impossible to determine exactly the longitude of ships or shores, because time pieces which functioned accurately at sea did not yet exist. This particular problem was solved only at the end of the 18th century when John Harrisson developed the chronometer.

In addition to sailing orders and sea charts, the directors gave the masters a trunk containing a large number of 'navigational tools', including several compasses with accessories, dividers, slide rule, binoculars, a celestial globe showing the most important constellations, and various instruments

to measure the altitude of the sun and the stars above the horizon. It is possible to calculate the geographical latitude on the basis of the altitude of the sun or stars. The round or semi-round astrolabe and the cross-staff are among the oldest altimeters. The davisquadrant and octant made their appearance in the 17th and 18th centuries respectively. Using a hand log and hourglass the seamen estimated the ship's speed and with a plumbline sounded the water's depth.
With these aids and appliances, some luck and a lot of common sense most VOC masters reached their Asian destination without accident. In the first years of the 17th century a small number of ships sailed from the Dutch Republic directly to Surat and the Coromandel Coast in India and, later, to Ceylon. In the 18th century the Gentlemen XVII sent some Company ships directly to Bengal and China. However, Batavia was by far the most common destination for VOC ships. After a passage of 15,000 miles lasting an average of eight months, they dropped anchor in the sheltered roadstead before the city. Should an East Indiaman have completed the voyage in less time, the fortunate officers received a bonus of 150 to 600 guilders, which they divided among themselves.

The final destination of most East Indiamen was Batavia on West- Java, the headquarters of the VOC in Asia.
Print by R. and J. Ottens 1730

Some East Indiamen spent most of their lives in Asia. After two unsuccessful attempts, the *Leiderdorp* finally left Texel at the end of 1771 for Batavia, where it was sold five years later. Anonymous drawing

The two visors on the case of the compass were used to take bearings to determine the position of the ship at sea.
Bearing compass by J. van Keulen end of the 17th century

With the conquest of the Portuguese in Malacca in 1641, the VOC gained control over the Strait of Malacca, an important trade route between West and East Asia. Anonymous drawing end of the 18th century

Mocha, located on the Red Sea, was a small settlement where the voc purchased Arabian coffee for the European market.
Chart in J. van Keulen, *De nieuwe groote lichtende zeefakkel* VI, Amsterdam 1753

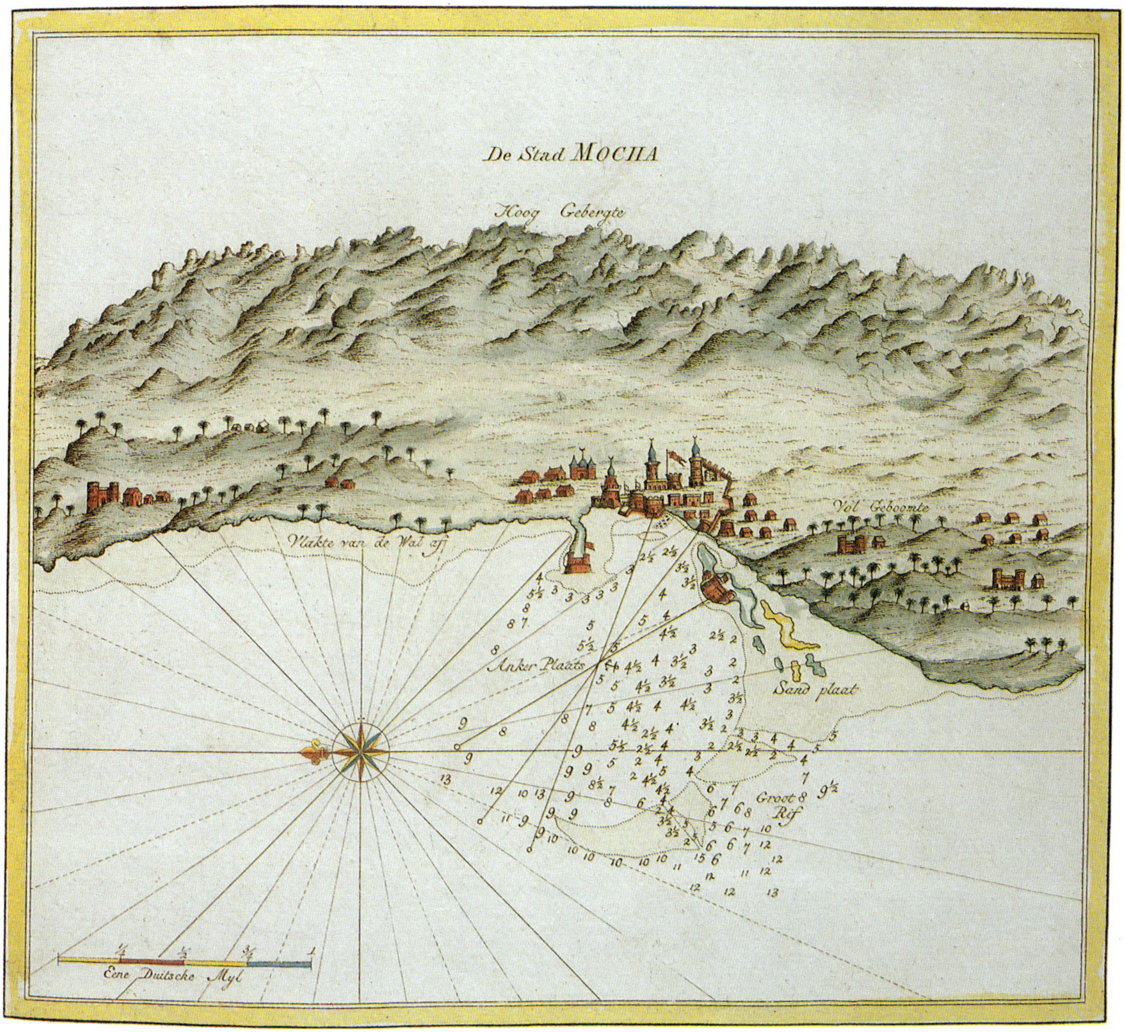

Following the example of other European companies, the voc established itself in Canton in the 18th century in order to purchase tea. All European trading posts were located along the Pearl River. Chinese export porcelain 1775

Settlements in Asia

Batavia, located on West Java, served as the voc headquarters in Asia and was the centre of an extensive Dutch trading network. The Company founded its own offices in various places along the important Asian trade routes to collect simpler products for Europe. The voc had insufficient means of exchange to purchase the coveted spices directly. European goods were often either too expensive for the Asian market or simply not in demand. Therefore, the Company, for example, sold silver imported from Europe in China. The profits were invested in Chinese silk that was shipped to Japan where it was traded for gold and copper. The Company then exported the Japanese goods to India, where it exchanged the gold and copper for textiles. The voc finally traded this Indian merchandise in the Moluccas for cloves, mace and nutmeg. It was an inexpensive way of acquiring Asian products that yielded high profits in Europe. The relatively small investment in silver multiplied through first purchasing silk, then gold and copper and consequently textiles in the production centres at a low price, and reselling them elsewhere in Asia, where they were in great demand, for a high profit.

The voc established its trade network using a combination of military force, commercial pressure and diplomacy. The Company's primary goal was to secure a monopoly on spices. This meant a bitter struggle with the Portuguese and other European competitors as well as local Asian populations who, according to the Dutch, did not honour their agreements. Mace and nutmeg, two spices from the same tree, were grown only on the Banda Islands. In 1602 the inhabitants promised to deliver the spices exclusively to the Dutch. However, they proceeded to break the agreement in all sorts of ways, because the voc was unable to provide them with food and clothing in exchange for the spices. In order to survive the Bandanese were forced to conduct business with Portuguese, English, Spanish and Asian merchants. Jan Pietersz Coen put an end to this 'smuggling' in 1621 in a grizzly fashion. He executed the most prominent Bandanese and murdered or deported a large part of the population. Those remaining fled into the mountains where the majority died of starvation. The voc built Fort Hollandia on a strategic site and laid out nutmeg plantations. The Company populated the Banda Islands with slaves and colonists who worked and managed the plantations. They were required to sell the entire harvest to the voc for a fixed price. This regulation remained in effect until 1864.

The monopoly on cloves was more difficult to obtain. Previously, this spice grew wild only on Makian, one of the northern Moluccas. The tremendous European demand stimulated the cultivation of cloves and tiny plants were brought to Ambon, Ceram and other southern Moluccas in hollow, earth-filled bamboo trunks. In 1600 and again in 1605 and 1607 the inhabitants of Ambon

In 1618 the VOC sent an expedition to the island of Boano north of Ambon to 'discipline' the inhabitants, 'the most wicked robbers in this entire region'.
Print in F. Valentijn, *Oud en nieuw Oost-Indien* II, Dordrecht 1724

and Ternate solemnly promised to supply their cloves exclusively to the Dutch. The VOC forced them to keep this promise by taking harsh actions which, as it turned out, were not very successful. Local rulers played off the Portuguese, Dutch, Spanish and English against each other. From 1625, the Company attempted to concentrate the cultivation of cloves on Ambon, the only island more or less under its control. It required each Ambonese head of family to plant and maintain ten clove trees. In addition, the VOC forced the Ambonese to undertake so-called *hongitochten*. These were expeditions with war-proas led by Company servants to other islands to chop down and burn clove trees. This measure was particularly effective, since clove trees only bear fruit after seven years. The VOC drove away the Portuguese and took over their forts. The Spanish retreated to the Philippines. The English East India Company left the Moluccas after the hasty execution – the so-called 'Amboina Massacre' – of ten English servants suspected of conspiring against the VOC. By 1650 the Company's grip on the clove trade was sufficient to supply the entire European market, but it was not until 1667, after a long struggle, that the large Asian spice port Macassar on Celebes fell into Dutch hands. For the time being the VOC possessed a valuable trade monopoly.

The Company launched other great military actions against the Portuguese on Ceylon, the most important cinnamon island, in Malabar on the southwest coast of India and on the Malay Peninsula. After long-lasting expeditions and innumerable blockades the territories fell to the Dutch. This gave the VOC a monopoly on cinnamon, a larger share of the pepper trade and the supervision of the Strait of Malacca, one of the most important trade routes between West and East Asia. Elsewhere the Company manifested

Between 1690 and 1781, Negapatnam was the headquarters for the voc settlements in Coromandel, the 1500 mile-long southeastern coast of India. Map of 1774

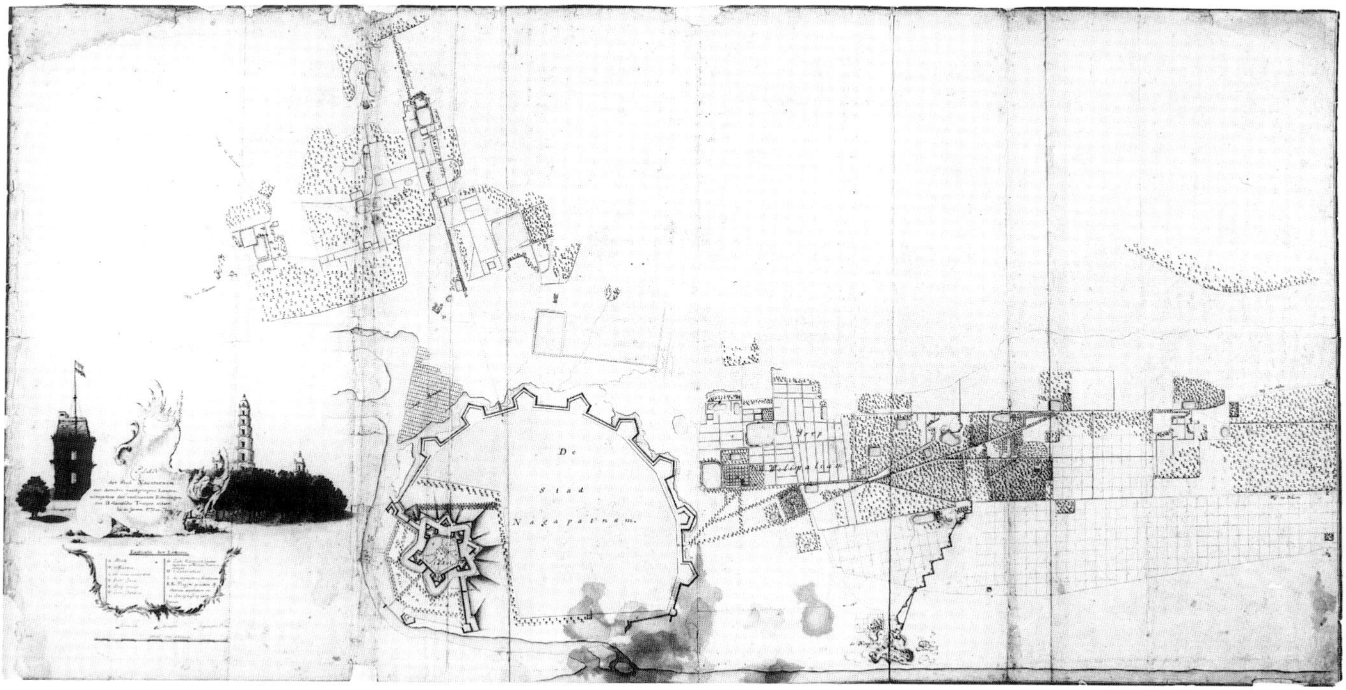

itself with less aggression. On Sumatra the voc concluded exclusive pepper contracts with rulers in Achin, Palembang and Jambi. The Company was unable to acquire a general pepper monopoly because pepper, in contrast to cloves, mace, nutmeg and cinnamon, was cultivated in a great many places in Asia.

The voc could not afford to use extensive aggression in India, China, Japan and Persia, because of the considerable might of the central governments. Then again, there was no great need for this, as the Company strove for limited trade aims that were subordinate to the spice monopoly. The voc negotiated with the representatives of the Great Mogul, the emperor of China, the shogun of Japan and the shah of Persia for advantageous trade privileges, or sent emissaries to the various courts with costly gifts in the hope of eliciting special promises from the omnipotent rulers. The Company requested exemption from, or a reduction in import and export duties, as well as permission to establish their own trading posts. The great rulers were prepared to extend privileges to the European merchants, because it was either financially or politically expedient for them to do so. The extensive fleet of the voc, its tremendous capital and, later, its monopoly of the spice trade were aspects which made the Company an attractive trading partner.

In India the voc established offices in Surat in the northwest, on the Coromandel Coast in the southeast and in Bengal in the northeast. Company servants did not live in fortified strongholds as they did in the Indonesian Archipelago, but often occupied nothing more than small dwellings with several warehouses in the centre of a busy seaport. On the market they were in direct competition with both Asian merchants and other Europeans. The voc also founded an office in Gamron on the Persian Gulf. In China it had limited success on Formosa. It was much simpler and cheaper to let Chinese junks transport the products to Batavia. After 1640, all Europeans except the Dutch were prohibited from conducting trade in Japan. To be sure, the Company was entirely dependent on the benevolence of the shogun and the voc servants were not allowed to leave the trading post on the small island of Deshima in the port of Nagasaki. Nevertheless, this situation was advantageous for the Dutch.

In the course of the 17th century the voc built up a trade network stretching from the Cape of Good Hope and Persia in the west, via India, Ceylon, Malacca and the Indonesian Archipelago to China and Japan in the far east. Batavia was the central crossroad founded by the voc with this purpose in mind. The Company wanted its headquarters and central warehouses to be built on private property. They had to be strategically located on the Sunda Strait or the Strait of Malacca, the main trade routes in Asia. In the beginning of the 17th century the Company used the international pepper port of Bantam, situated on the western-most point of Java. However, the local ruler refused to grant the voc special privileges and the Company was forced to tolerate the presence of Asian and other European competitors. For reasons of safety, in 1610 the voc built a fortified warehouse east of Bantam near Jacatra. This undertaking soon led to conflicts between the prince of Jacatra and ruler of Bantam. The voc emerged victorious from this squabble. In 1619 Jan Pietersz Coen built Fort Batavia on the former site of Jacatra. The fort grew into a veritable Dutch city in the tropics, intersected by canals for the irrigation of the surrounding swampland. The city was so unhealthy that, when ailing seamen reached its hospital at the end of their long passage from the Netherlands, they often died anyway. Around 1700 Batavia's population was 70,000. By the end of the 18th century this number had more than doubled. Approximately 6000 inhabitants were of European origin and the city was defended by 1200 soldiers.

The High Government or Council of the Indies, the highest governing body of the voc in Asia, had its seat in Batavia. The governor-general chaired the Council which answered only to the Gentlemen xvii. However, due to the eight month delay in relaying instructions to Asia, the directors had virtually no direct influence on business matters there. The High Government coordinated all of the Company's maritime, administrative and business affairs in Asia. It recounted new developments to the Gentlemen xvii in a general annual report or 'general missive'. Each year this body also drew up the 'general call', a list of cash and commodities that the Asian settlements wanted to receive from the Dutch Republic. The High Government based the general missive and call on information and requests it received from the VOC offices in Asia. Each settlement was headed by a governor, director, commander, resident or chief who, together with a Policy Council, managed the local affairs of the VOC. A senior merchant of the Company, the garrison commander, the bookkeeper and counsel had seats on the Council.

The extensive trade network, encompassing some thirty settlements, made the VOC the most powerful merchant in Asia and the largest trading company in the world at the end of the 17th century. It had a great advantage over its competitors. The Company disposed over silver in Japan, Persia and Europe. Furthermore, it was in a position to compare prices and the quality of goods. On the basis of such information the VOC bought raw silk in Bengal, China or Persia and shipped it to Japan or Europe. Not the least of its market advantages, the Company held the monopoly on spices. It purchased cloves, mace, nutmeg and cinnamon for extremely low prices and sold them in Europe at great profit. Finally, the VOC earned a great deal of money with trade conducted between its Asian settlements.

During the 18th century, however, the enormous Asian network became an increasingly heavy burden for the Company. It had to maintain its advantageous trade position against European competitors and defend its possessions from attacks launched by Asian rulers. The VOC therefore sent an increasing number of civil servants and soldiers overseas. Around 1625 the number of servants in the Asian branch of the Company was barely 2500. At the end of the 17th century, their number had risen to 13,000. By 1750, 20,000 civil servants and soldiers populated the Company's Asian settlements. This caused costs to increase at an alarming rate while revenues decreased. Japan limited foreign trade and the Persian empire experienced chaos. The VOC lost its Asian sources of precious metals. The spice monopoly yielded fewer advantages, because Europeans purchased more Indian textiles and Chinese tea than cloves, mace, nutmeg, cinnamon and pepper. English merchants surpassed the VOC in China and India. The Company lost much of its influence in Surat, Malabar, Coromandel and Bengal, but expanded its power on Ceylon and Java. The VOC established vast coffee and sugar plantations in the region surrounding Batavia and on East Java. These shifts meant that the Company became much more of an administrator than a merchant. The VOC ultimately withdrew to the islands of the Indonesian Archipelago, which later became the Dutch East Indies.

The Company maintained contact between the various settlements in Asia with its own ships. Most of the large East Indiamen arriving from Europe served several months in Asia before returning home. The ships were serviced and repaired in Batavia in the shipyards, which the Company had introduced on the various islands off the coast. On Onrust (Turmoil), Kuiper (Cooper) and Edam there were slipways, forges, sawmills, a pulley and sailmaker's shop and a ropewalk where convicts served hard labour. Batavia boasted the best-equipped repair shipyard in Asia well into the 19th century. Sometimes the VOC had small ships built. The greatest problem was finding adequate building materials, the majority of which had to be supplied from Europe and frequently arrived in poor condition. In addition, the Company contended with a shortage of skilled craftsmen.

The rhythm of the monsoons governed shipping within Asia. The ships sailed from the roadstead of Batavia to Japan between May and June, to the Moluccas between November and February, to Bengal and the Coromandel Coast between July and August and to Ceylon and further west between August and September. The Company selected the vessels on the basis of their soundness. The newest and best East Indiamen collected the valuable Bengal and Japanese products. The old, virtually discarded ships spent their last years along the sheltered north coast of Java. The masters received the material necessary for their Asian routes from the chief mapmaker in Batavia. The VOC settlements, situated on dangerous coasts or inland along rivers, employed their own pilots to steer the large East Indiamen into the anchorage. The ship's crew, together with Asian helpers, unloaded the cargoes in small lighters, often simply local fishing boats. In Coromandel, the Company used *thonijs*, a type of rowing/sailing boat and in Surat *horrys*, a kind of bluff-bowed sailing vessel. On the north coast of Java the VOC loaded and unloaded its goods with *pantjallings*. From all over Asia the products were brought to Batavia, the Company's official depot or 'rendez-vous'. From there, the VOC distributed the goods to its various settlements and to Europe.

The Dutch were the only Europeans allowed to trade with Japan between 1641 and 1853. Twelve VOC servants lived in isolation on the small island of Deshima. Detail of a Japanese drawing 18th century

Kazimbazar was one of the VOC trading posts in Bengal where the Company purchased large quantities of raw silk.
Painting by H. Schuylenburgh 1665 (Loan Rijksmuseum Amsterdam)

Between 1602 and 1799 the VOC maintained a total of approximately thirty settlements in Asia. However, the Company was established on Formosa only in the 17th century, and in Canton and on Borneo in the 18th century.

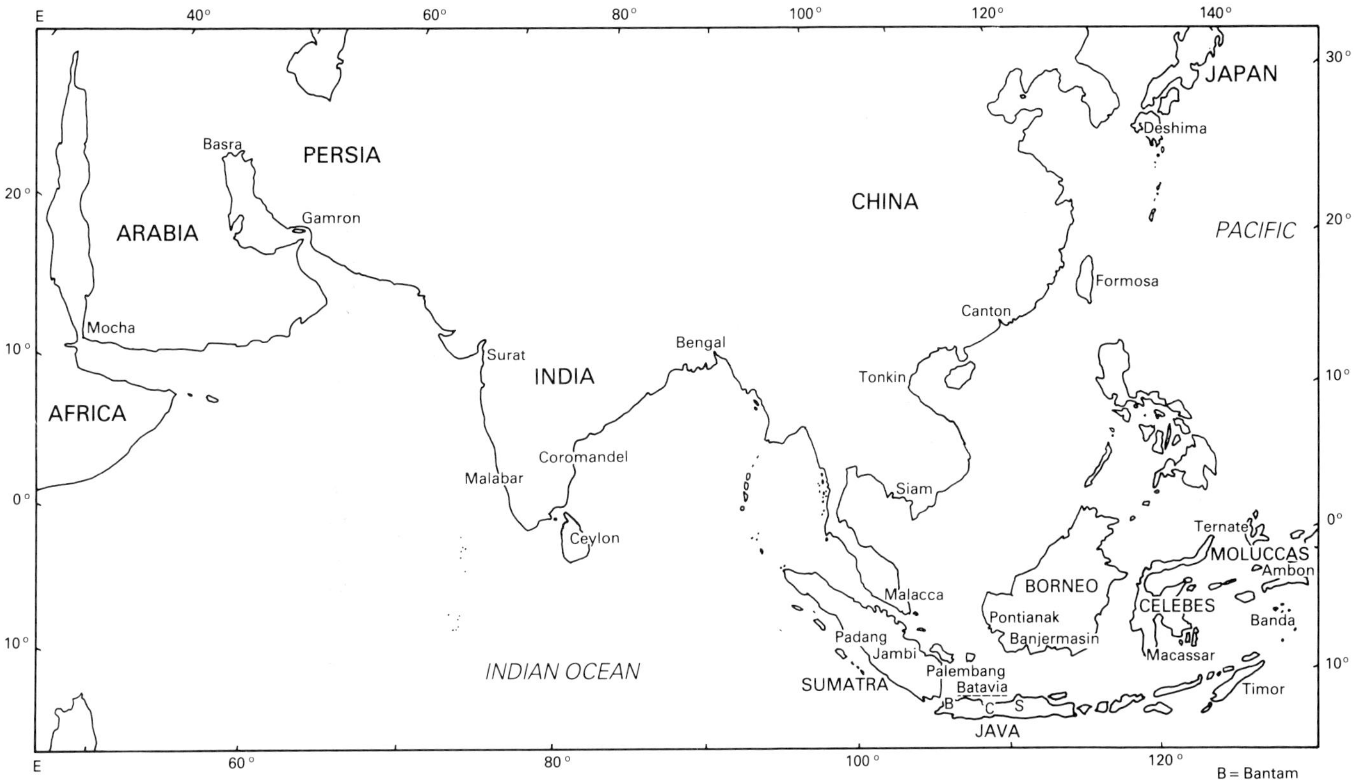

B = Bantam

C = Cheribon

S = Semarang

Japanese coolies, hired by the Company on a temporary basis, loaded and unloaded the trade goods on Deshima. Detail of an anonymous Japanese drawing

Asian Products

The voc traded in more than a hundred different Asian goods. In the 17th century pepper and other spices were the most important products. They comprised almost sixty percent of all the cargoes shipped to Europe, where they yielded high profits. Pepper grew in many places in Asia. The voc bought Sumatran pepper in Palembang and Bantam and Malabar pepper on the southwestern coast of India, shipping an average of 6 million pounds to Europe every year. The Company disposed of another 3 million pounds within Asia, in China and India. With the profit, the voc then bought other Asian products for export to Europe. The finer spices, cloves, mace and nutmeg came from the Moluccas. The Asian population and the European colonists cultivated the clove and nutmeg trees, delivering the harvest for a fixed price to the Company each year. Although the most important outlet was Europe, the voc also sold cloves in Surat and elsewhere in India. The Company collected large quantities of the best-quality cinnamon in Ceylon. A separate caste of cinnamon peelers annually produced a pre-determined quantity of cinnamon per person for a fixed price. Supervised by a Cinnamon Captain the peelers trekked into the forests and stripped the bark from the trees in long bands. The bark was dried in the sun which caused the strips to curl up into long sticks. There was only a very small market for cinnamon in Asia. The annual harvest of approximately 4 million pounds was almost

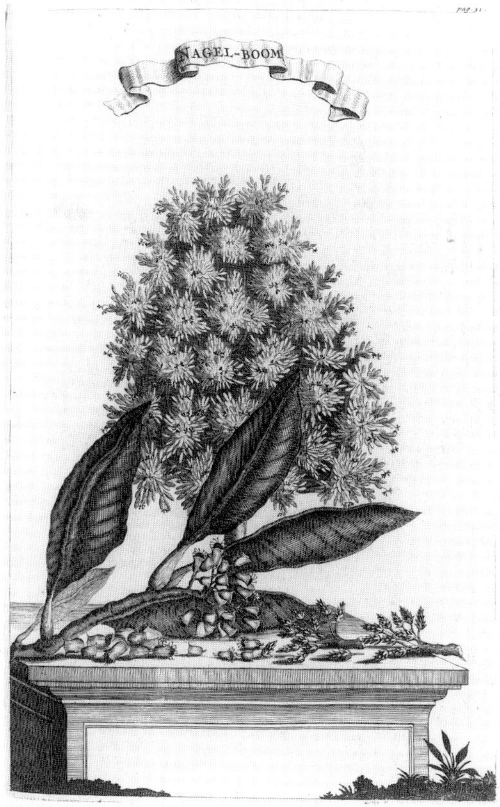

A clove tree on a pedestal emphasizes the importance of spices for the voc.
Print in J. Nieuhof, *Gedenckwaerdige zee- en lantreize*, Amsterdam 1682

entirely shipped to the Dutch Republic. In Europe the spices were added to bland food to make it more appetizing. They were ingredients used in mulled wine and saffron milk, a beverage made of saffron, cloves, cinnamon and mace mixed with sugar and cooked in milk. Europeans also used spices for medicinal purposes to treat all sorts of complaints. Thus, in the Dutch Republic both grocery stores and apothecaries sold spices.
Within Asia, the Company also traded in Japanese copper and precious metals. In Bengal and on the Coromandel Coast there was a great demand for copper to be converted into coinage. In addition the Indians used copper for making statues of Buddha, temple decorations, utensils, tools and as roof covering. In many places in Asia the Japanese precious metal was a welcome addition to the trade goods the VOC supplied. In Bengal the Company profitably converted Japanese silver bars into sicca rupees, the local currency, with which it could purchase fabric. For the same purpose, Japanese gold coins, kobans, were melted down into pagodas on the Coromandel Coast. The VOC collected smaller quantities of gold in Timor, Sumatra, Malacca and China. In the second half of the 17th century Japan limited the export of precious metals. This was a severe loss for the Company. As compensation the VOC purchased European silver and gold coins in Persia. Venetian and Hungarian ducats as well as other European coins reached the Persian market via long caravan routes. Merchants brought Persian silk overland to the Mediterranean. They were paid with European currency with which they bought Asian products, primarily pepper and other spices, from the VOC in Persia. The Company itself also traded in raw silk. It shipped the silk from Persia, Bengal and China to Japan and exchanged it for copper, gold and silver. In addition Europe was a major outlet in the 17th century. Asian raw silk replaced Italian silk as the basic material for the European silk industry.

The assortment of VOC goods changed at the end of the 17th century. The share of spices decreased to one-third, even though their volume remained generally the same. From then on, vast quantities of less profitable Indian piece goods filled the holds. In the 17th century the VOC traded in Indian cottons in order to acquire spices on the Moluccas. In the 18th century a great demand for Indian textiles also emerged in Europe, including cottons, silk and mixed fabrics of cotton and silk from Bengal, the Coromandel Coast and Surat. The textiles came in a wide range of sizes and were available in solids, stripes and checks. It was not easy for the Company servants to distinguish among the various sorts of doreas, rumals or kerchiefs, mulmuls, fotas, guinea cloths, baftas, betillas, niquanias, parcals or salampuris. Famous are the Coromandel chintzes with their colorful patterns, dyed, painted or printed. Indian textiles were used in the Dutch Republic for table cloths, bedspreads, curtains and clothing. Dutch traditional costumes and the multi-coloured peasant kerchiefs still bear motifs of Indian origin.
In the 18th century tea and coffee became popular beverages in Europe. Tea and coffee houses proliferated. This occasionally caused difficulties for beer brewers. The market for tea in the 17th century was limited as it was recommended as a remedy for headaches, among other ailments. The VOC had the dried leaves brought in junks from China to Batavia. The Company adhered to this ancient practice even when the demand for tea increased. Other Europeans, however, sailed directly to China. They bought a better quality tea from the Chinese for a lower price than the VOC

This small Japanese medicine bottle, decorated with Dutch musicians, was one of the trinkets, which the VOC shipped to Europe in small quantities (18th century).

was able to in Batavia. The Company opened up a direct route to China only at the end of the 1720s. By then it had already lost the battle for control of the European tea market. In the 18th century the consumption of coffee was so widespread that 'the maids and seamstresses have to have their coffee in the morning, or they are unable to thread their needles'. The Arabian coffee available in Europe in the 17th century was too expensive. This led the VOC to successfully establish coffee plantations on Java and force the local population to deliver the harvest to the Company. The cost of Javanese coffee for the VOC was thus one-tenth of that of Arabian coffee. As a result of the low prices the potential markets in Europe expanded.
Within Asia the Company conducted a lucrative trade in opium, the concentrated juice of the poppy plant. In fact, the VOC had a monopoly on trade in opium well into the 18th century. In Bengal it bought up practically the entire harvest. The Company brought the 'sleeping gum' to Batavia where it was sold to Asian merchants at a great profit. In turn, these merchants sold the opium in the Indonesian Archipelago or shipped it to China, even though the Chinese Government officially banned its import. In Bengal, the Company also bought saltpetre, thin salt crystals which grow like frost on dry hot ground. It was a profitable ballast cargo for the homeward-bound voyage, since there were good potential markets in Europe for saltpetre as it was the primary ingredient in gunpowder. The Company collected large quantities of tin in Malacca, Siam and, in the 18th century, on Banka Island, off the east coast of Sumatra. An almost insatiable demand for tin existed in China. The Chinese made a kind of tin foil which they burnt daily as little offertory papers. In addition, great quantities of tin were required to line tea-chests to preserve the fragrance

and flavour of the tea during the long trip to Europe. On Java the VOC's own plantations supplied inexpensive sugar, which the Company disposed of within Asia in Surat, Malabar and Persia. In Europe the Javanese product had to compete with West Indian sugar.

Other VOC trade goods included dyes, such as indigo, and goat hair for the millinery shop in Batavia, as well as innumerable trinkets: gifts from Asian princes, Ceylonese elephants, Persian horses, Indian diamonds, Japanese lacquerwork and Chinese porcelain. The 'Japanese coat', a type of kimono, was long popular in Europe as a dressing gown for gentlemen of standing. The present-day Dutch 'japon' (dress) is a simple descendant of the stately dressing gown.

Before becoming governor-general of the Indies in 1681, Cornelis Speelman (1628-1684) held voc positions in Coromandel, Macassar and the Molucca Islands. Anonymous painting end of the 17th century

The voc traded in hundreds of kinds of Indian textiles. This bedspread made of cotton chintz from Coromandel displays a mixture of Indian and European motifs. (Fries Museum Leeuwarden)

In 1720 commander Michiel Landsheer returned to the Dutch Republic safe and sound with a return fleet of 19 ships from Batavia and Ceylon.
Anonymous drawing

In 1784 four large men-of-war and two frigates under the command of Van Braam freed besieged Malacca with a landing near Teluk Ketapang. Painting by E. Hoogerheyden 1800

The Return Fleet

The voc collected the goods in its warehouses both in Batavia and on the little islands off the coast. The ships were loaded in the roadstead. Heavy ballast goods, such as saltpetre or sugar were placed in the bottom and covered with mats; then came a layer of pepper in bags, which was also covered. Bales of textiles rested on this lower layer. Simple fabrics were stored lower, and the more expensive ones higher in the ship. The spaces between the bundles were filled with loose pepper or chips of sapanwood, the raw material for making red dye. Raw silk and other valuable goods were stored underneath the quarterdeck. The provisions were stowed between the decks.

On the evening before departure, the master and the officers held a lavish farewell dinner. The East Indiamen could leave Batavia during any season, with easterly or westerly monsoons. At the beginning of the 17th century the ships set sail the moment their holds had been loaded. Due to the circumstances of war, however, it became necessary to navigate European waters in convoy. Thus, the homeward-bounders sailed as a fleet from Asia to the Dutch Republic. Initially, a Christmas fleet set out at the end of December, followed in mid-January by several 'after ships'. Later, three to four smaller fleets left the roadstead of Batavia between October and February. The voc appointed a commander of the fleet who wielded the highest authority during the return voyage. This was an honorary position bestowed upon high-ranking Company servants who were returning to the Dutch Republic, either because they were entitled to a leave of absence or had completed their term of employment. When leaving the roadstead, the crewmen who had been favoured to man the return fleet sang at the top of their lungs: 'Farewell Batavia, we're now sailing home' as a parting gesture. The ships sailed through the Sunda Strait toward the south. The southeast trade wind led the East Indiamen over the shortest route across the Indian Ocean to the Cape. The cyclones raging in the area surrounding the island of Mauritius between January and March were a tremendous threat. Between 1720 and 1740 nineteen voc ships were swallowed up by the waves. As a result, in 1742 the Gentlemen xvii altered sailing instructions for the return voyages. Henceforth, the homeward-bounders departed from Batavia in two fleets; the first left in September, the second at the end of January to ensure that the East Indiamen would no longer be in the vicinity of Mauritius during the treacherous months.

On the return passage the Company ships stopped at the Cape to repair the fleet. After a voyage across the Indian Ocean lasting two to three months, restocking was less urgent. Homeward-bounders from all parts of Asia joined the Batavian fleet. Since its conquest of Ceylon from the Portuguese, the voc ships sailed directly from the island to the Dutch Republic in order to transport

The model of the East Indiaman *Ary* was supposedly built for Czar Peter the Great as an example for Russian shipbuilders. However, the czar died before the ship was completed. The new owner must have named the model after himself, a friend or relative since the VOC never had a ship named *Ary*.

the Indian products, particularly the perishable cinnamon, more quickly to Europe. Batavia fiercely resisted this attempt to undermine its position as the VOC's staple market in Asia. Ceylon did not have sufficient supplies or facilities for repairing ships. Furthermore, the VOC governor of Ceylon would not have been able to supervise matters properly. The Gentlemen XVII were swayed by the arguments and limited these 'direct consignments'. Nonetheless, when Indian textiles and Chinese tea became the most important trade commodities in the 18th century, the directors re-established a direct route to Ceylon, Bengal, the Coromandel Coast and Canton. The merchandise reached the European market faster and in better condition.

Once at the Cape of Good Hope the ships awaited instructions from the Gentlemen XVII concerning the route to be followed to the Dutch Republic. From the Cape the return fleet set course in the direction of Saint Helena, which stood out like a beacon in the middle of the Atlantic Ocean. Passing Ascension Island and the Azores, the ships sailed either to the Channel or the backway around Scotland, depending on the instructions. On the homeward-bound passage the long northern route was not very popular. In order to motivate the crew to take this route when necessary, all those on board were offered a bonus of two to three months extra wages upon their arrival home. At the entrance of the Channel or near the Shetland Islands, VOC cruisers and several men-of-war awaited the return fleet to escort it on the last leg of the voyage. The Company ships made their final stop in their individual home ports. In times of hardship – war or serious autumn storms – they had to steer for the closest safe port. This procedure sometimes raised protests. In 1672, during the Third Anglo-Dutch

War, the Middelburg guilds accused the Zeeland director, De Muncq, of 'treason', because he had permitted three Zeeland homeward-bounders to be unloaded and consequently equipped at Texel. The return fleet had fled, however, by sailing around Scotland to Bergen in Norway. De Ruyter cunningly piloted the ships passed the English blockade, bringing them to Texel. This manoeuvre robbed the Middelburg small businessmen of much income. The severe accusations they launched at De Muncq illustrates the Company's tremendous involvement in the local economy of the cities and regions where its chambers were located.

After the return voyage of 13,400 miles lasting on average seven-and-a-half months, the homeward-bounders dropped anchor, usually during summer, in the roadsteads of Rammekens, Goeree or Texel. The directors of the Department of the Equipage boarded the ships for inspection. They discharged the crew from their oath of loyalty to the Company. With only a small bundle of clothing under their arm the seamen were taken to shore in lighters. They could collect their sea chests in the East India House after inspection together with the profit of the permitted goods, which the VOC auctioned on their behalf. The commander of the return fleet reported to the directors of the presiding chamber, Amsterdam or Zeeland, and then to the States-General in The Hague. On that occasion the commander received an 'honour' in the form of a silver or gold medallion chain valuing 500 to 1000 guilders.

After the cargoes had been unloaded, the ships were brought to the dock where they were unrigged and repaired. The Asian products were carefully sorted in the Company's warehouses. Each chamber published a detailed list of the merchandise to be auctioned. While most of the products appeared on the market during the autumn auctions, the Company sold the spices in the spring. At the beginning of the 17th century the VOC delivered the most important products on contract to regular groups of merchants, often the directors themselves. The Company did not sell the products on the open market thus the merchants profited from the monopoly of the VOC. The sales became public as of 1642 and also acquired an international character. Buyers were allowed to sample the products in the warehouses a week before the auction. Brokers inspected the wares and recorded their judgments on quality in small printed books with lot numbers. The VOC

'Jan de With as commander of the homeward-bounders...in the year 1746 delivered to the harbours of these countries, was...with this [gold] medallion chain...honoured in memory'.

After unloading their cargo, the Amsterdam East Indiamen returned to the Company shipyard on the IJ for repairs and cleaning. Drawing by H. Kobell 1776

On 29 October 1689 five homeward-bounders arrived 'before the city of Vere (Thank God)'. Among the goods on board were 1.5 million pounds of pepper and thousands of pieces of Indian textiles.

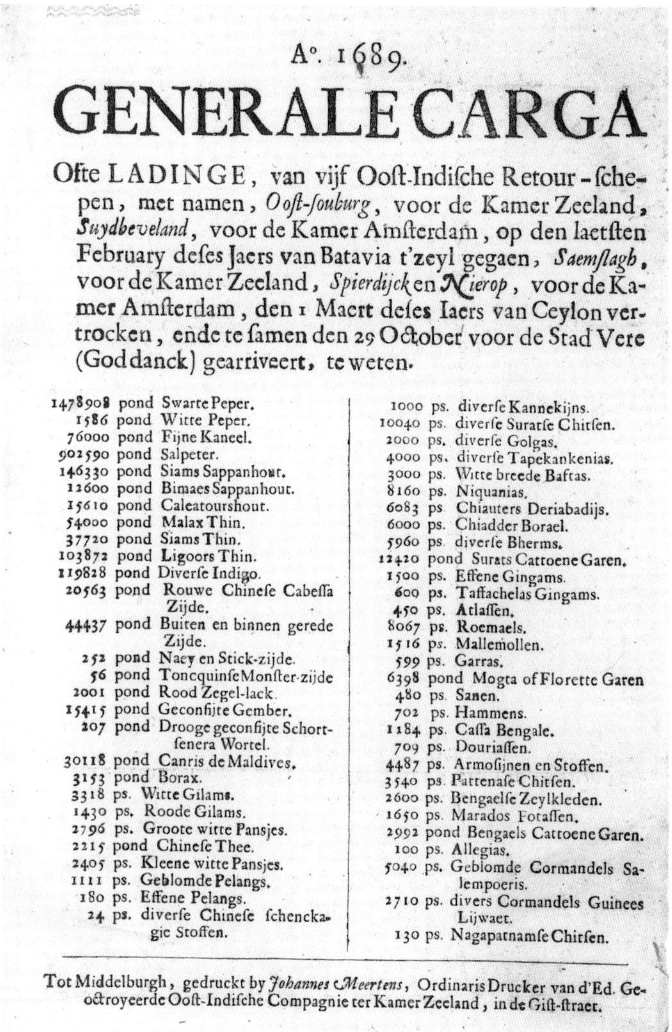

A°. 1689.

GENERALE CARGA

Ofte LADINGE, van vijf Ooſt-Indiſche Retour-ſchepen, met namen, *Ooſt-Souburg*, voor de Kamer Zeeland, *Suydbeveland*, voor de Kamer Amſterdam, op den laetſten February deſes Jaers van Batavia t'zeyl gegaen, *Saemſlagh*, voor de Kamer Zeeland, *Spierdijck* en *Nierop*, voor de Kamer Amſterdam, den 1 Maert deſes Iaers van Ceylon vertrocken, ende te ſamen den 29 October voor de Stad Vere (Goddanck) gearriveert, te weten.

1478908	pond	Swarte Peper.
1586	pond	Witte Peper.
76000	pond	Fijne Kaneel.
902590	pond	Salpeter.
146330	pond	Siams Sappanhout.
12600	pond	Bimaes Sappanhout.
15610	pond	Caleatourshout.
54000	pond	Malax Thin.
37720	pond	Siams Thin.
103872	pond	Ligoors Thin.
119828	pond	Diverſe Indigo.
20563	pond	Rouwe Chineſe Cabeſſa Zijde.
44437	pond	Buiten en binnen gerede Zijde.
252	pond	Naey en Stick-zijde.
56	pond	Toncquinſe Monſter-zijde
2001	pond	Rood Zegel-lack.
15415	pond	Geconfijte Gember.
207	pond	Drooge geconfijte Schortſenera Wortel.
30118	pond	Canris de Maldives.
3153	pond	Borax.
3318	ps.	Witte Gilams.
1430	ps.	Roode Gilams.
2796	ps.	Groote witte Panſjes.
2215	pond	Chineſe Thee.
2405	ps.	Kleene witte Panſjes.
1111	ps.	Geblomde Pelangs.
180	ps.	Effene Pelangs.
24	ps.	diverſe Chineſe ſchenckagie Stoffen.
1000	ps.	diverſe Kannekijns.
10040	ps.	diverſe Suratſe Chitſen.
2000	ps.	diverſe Golgas.
4000	ps.	diverſe Tapekankenias.
3000	ps.	Witte breede Baftas.
8160	ps.	Niquanias.
6083	ps.	Chiauters Deriabadijs.
6000	ps.	Chiadder Borael.
5960	ps.	diverſe Bherms.
12420	pond	Surats Cattoene Garen.
1500	ps.	Effene Gingams.
600	ps.	Taffachelas Gingams.
450	ps.	Atlaſſen.
8067	ps.	Roemaels.
1516	ps.	Mallemollen.
599	ps.	Garras.
6398	pond	Mogta of Florette Garen
480	ps.	Sanen.
702	ps.	Hammens.
1184	ps.	Caſſa Bengale.
709	ps.	Douriaſſen.
4487	ps.	Armoſijnen en Stoffen.
3540	ps.	Pattenaſe Chitſen.
2600	ps.	Bengaelſe Zeylkleden.
1650	ps.	Marados Fotaſſen.
2992	pond	Bengaels Cattoene Garen.
100	ps.	Allegias.
5040	ps.	Geblomde Cormandels Salempoeris.
2710	ps.	divers Cormandels Guinees Lijwaet.
130	ps.	Nagapatnamſe Chitſen.

Tot Middelburgh, gedruckt by *Johannes Meertens*, Ordinaris Drucker van d'Ed. Geoctroyeerde Ooſt-Indiſche Compagnie ter Kamer Zeeland, in de Giſt-ſtraet.

distributed an extensive catalogue of 150 to 200 pages containing specific information on quality, measurements and patterns of the Indian textiles. The sales began at 9 a.m., led by an auctioneer, and were held in the presence of several directors, the secretary of the city and a few clerks. As a rule, thirty to forty brokers and important merchants gathered in the auction hall of the East India House.

After the auction the buyers drew up their own invoices, which they then presented for inspection to the directors of the Department of Commerce. They received a reduction if they paid immediately. But if payment was delayed, the directors charged interest, warehouse rent and storage fees. The buyer was required to turn over one-thousandth of the total amount to the local poor relief fund. After having settled the bill at the exchange bank, the buyer received printed proof of payment with which he could collect his goods at the VOC warehouse. Then, finally, in for example the autumn of 1682 or spring of 1683 Asian products reached the European market, which the Gentlemen XVII had put on their provisional list of orders two years earlier, in September 1680. They sent their request around Christmas of 1680 to Batavia, where it arrived between May and August of 1681. The headquarters parcelled out the orders to the Company's various Asian settlements. At best the goods reached Batavia in time to be shipped to the Dutch Republic in December of 1681 or January of 1682, where they ultimately arrived in the summer. Following this long supply route the VOC delivered Asian products to Europe for two centuries. Their collective purchase price was almost 1 billion guilders. Sales in the Dutch Republic alone yielded the Company more than 2.5 billion guilders.

The Collapse

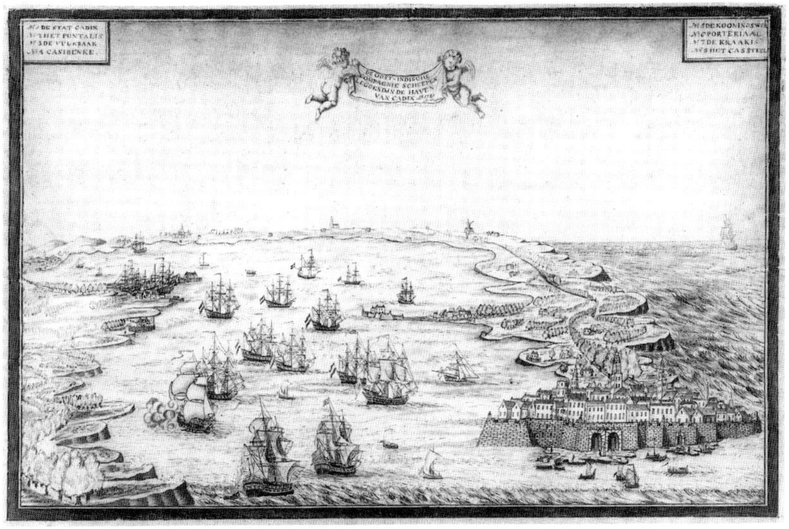

In 1781 the return fleet of commander Kornelis Kornelissen fled from the English to the port of Cadiz. The VOC sold the ships later in Marseilles.
Drawing by P. Luypen 1781

In the 17th and 18th century the VOC was the largest trading and shipping company in the world. The Company employed thousands of people, owned some thirty settlements in Asia and six chambers in the Dutch Republic, as well as a fleet of more than one hundred ships. At the end of the 18th century, however, this multinational enterprise went bankrupt. The directors were simply not prepared for demands which the immense company, the tremendous distances and the long-term planning placed on them. The convoluted bookkeeping and the six departments in the Dutch Republic did not make running the Company efficiently and effectively any easier. Moreover, inadequate financing coupled with insufficient capital stock and too many short-term loans made the Company vulnerable. In Asia, expenses increased while revenues decreased. The VOC had to defend its lucrative trade position and extensive possessions from European competitors and Asian rulers. The shift in the selection of goods destined for Europe proved disadvantageous for the Company. The cheap, mass-produced products, in which the VOC could hardly compete with other merchants, yielded lower profits than the expensive spices on which the Company held the monopoly. Fraudulent tampering with weights or quality as well as private trading by employees, which was strictly prohibited, injured the VOC. Little evidence exists, however, to prove that the corruption and smuggling which took place in the 18th century occurred any less frequently in the 17th century.

Under such conditions the VOC could no longer withstand the effects of the Fourth Anglo-Dutch War. The English privateered a large number of homeward-bounders and confiscated various settlements in Asia. Dutch trade lay dormant for two years. The Company fell into serious debt. Only with considerable government support could it hope to surmount its problems. A navy squadron under the command of Jan Pieter van Braam sailed to Asia, but was unable to do much for the Company. The States-General extended considerable financial support. Given the tremendous economic interests involved, the States of Holland also were prepared to issue sizeable loans. The collapse of the Company would have proved disastrous for the cities where the chambers were located.

Nevertheless, the voc was trapped in a vicious circle. Despite the tremendous financial support it received, the Company still did not have enough money to send a sufficient number of ships and personnel to Asia. Thus, it was unable to purchase enough Asian products whereby revenues in the Dutch Republic were too small to counterbalance the alarming shortage of personnel and ships. The French invasion of the Dutch Republic and the dismissal of Stadholder-Prince William V in 1795 signaled the beginning of the end for the Company. The directors were replaced by a Committee for the Affairs of the East India Trade and Possessions. At the end of 1799 the mammoth company was nationalised and the Dutch Government assumed all its debts and possessions. The monopoly rights, however, were retained for some products. Dutch shipping to Asia continued much as it had, though under a different name and flag. In 1803 the Chambers of Delft, Hoorn and Enkhuizen were dissolved and those of Middelburg and Rotterdam were demoted to sales agencies. The employees were discharged, all the shipyards were dismantled and, in so far as possible, handed over to the navy. It was a quiet and sad ending for such an illustrious trading company.

The grain merchants Cruys and Beerenbroek bought the Amsterdam East India Entrepot in 1820. Two years later the warehouse collapsed with a thundering crash under the weight of heavy loads of grain.
Print by C. de Kruyf en J. Lutz 1822